MW01275055

UNDERSTANDING SCHOOL CHOICE IN CANADA

Understanding School Choice in Canada

LYNN BOSETTI AND DIANNE GERELUK

UNIVERSITY OF TORONTO PRESS
Toronto Buffalo London

ISBN 978-1-4426-4308-6

Library and Archives Canada Cataloguing in Publication

Bosetti, Lynn, 1959–, author
Understanding school choice in Canada / Lynn Bosetti and Dianne Gereluk.

Includes bibliographical references and index.
ISBN 978-1-4426-4308-6 (cloth)

1. School choice – Canada.   I. Gereluk, Dianne, author   II. Title.

LB1027.9.B68 2016   379.1'110971   C2016-900799-5

University of Toronto Press acknowledges the financial assistance to
its publishing program of the Canada Council for the Arts and the Ontario Arts
Council, an agency of the Government of Ontario.

Canada Council
for the Arts

Conseil des Arts
du Canada

ONTARIO ARTS COUNCIL
CONSEIL DES ARTS DE L'ONTARIO
an Ontario government agency
un organisme du gouvernement de l'Ontario

Funded by the
Government
of Canada

Financé par le
gouvernement
du Canada

Canadä

In memory of my father, Dr. Reno Bosetti, who was vigilant in his support for public education.

Lynn Bosetti

To my mother, Eileen Makowecki, who continues to inspire me each and every single day.

Dianne Gereluk

Contents

List of Tables   ix

Acknowledgments   xi

Introduction   3

1 Philosophical Frameworks for Understanding School Choice
in Canada   15

2 Educational Accommodations for National Minority Groups   32
WRITTEN WITH DAVID SCOTT

3 Educational Accommodations for Other Minority Groups   50

4 Evolution of School Choice in Canada and the Rise of Parental
Rights and Freedoms   70

5 School Choice as Concerted Cultivation: Middle-Class Anxiety
and Advantage   94

6 Ethical Principles to Guide School Choice Policies in Canada   112

References   141

Index   163

Tables

1   Distribution of Anglophone, Francophone, and French
    Immersion Schools   47
2   Provincial and Territorial Funding Levels for Faith-Based
    Schools across Canada   62
3   Provincial and Territorial Heritage-Language Program
    Funding   65
4   School Choice in Canada   80
5   Independent School Enrolment, 2009–2010   86

Acknowledgments

We are grateful for the significant contributions of many individuals who openly shared their vision, underpinning values, and perspectives on schooling. For more than 20 years we have talked with educators, administrators, superintendents, and government officials about the nature of school choice in alternative public schools, charter schools, and independent schools. Their willingness to articulate the ideals, barriers, and opportunities associated with school choice continues to remind us of the complexity of providing such educational alternatives.

We also want to thank the University of Toronto Press editorial board for their ongoing support and the constructive feedback we received from our blind reviewers. Their insightful recommendations pushed us to examine the nuances related to school choice policies in Canada. In the final revisions, we are particularly thankful to David Scott for his excellent editorial guidance. His subject matter expertise concerning the pluralist nature of Canada was particularly evident in his authored contributions to Chapter 2.

Finally, we want to thank our families for their support through this writing journey. While our growth as authors has been challenging and worthwhile, we recognize its cost in terms of quality time spent with our families. We thank you for your love and support.

UNDERSTANDING SCHOOL CHOICE IN CANADA

Introduction

School choice policies are prominently placed on most educational agendas in Western liberal democracies. The idea of choice is attractive. Its promise of equality, freedom, and democracy resonates with many political and social movements, and reflects the modern desire for autonomy, control, and self-expression (Forsey, Davies, & Walford, 2008). Debates around school choice policies can elicit strong, often emotional responses, spawning heated debates regarding the public and private purpose of schooling and its role in a democratic society. Provisions for school choice represent a shift in how citizens think about public education and how it is organized. The rationale for choice involves "reconfiguring the very terms 'public' and 'private' by expanding and reshaping what counts as public education" (T. Wilson, 2012, p. 17). In its most basic form, school choice involves giving parents the right to choose approaches to education beyond those offered through the school assigned to their children based on their neighbourhood. It requires school boards to respond to diverse needs and perspectives on how children should be educated, rather than agreeing on a particular form of curricula or provision for schooling.

Debates around school choice policies are often taken up in opposition to, or alongside, traditional conceptions of public schooling historically based on the common school model, despite the fact that Canada has a long history of publically funded separate Catholic and Protestant school systems and federally funded schools for Aboriginal students. This compulsory model of education brought a diverse population together in state-funded schools in an attempt to forge a common schooling experience that would help students acquire the necessary skills and knowledge to participate in the labour market and become productive members of society. The common schooling model has been upheld as a "crucible of citizenship, equal opportunity, and social cohesion" (Gaskell, 2001, p. 19; Barlow & Robertson, 1994; Gaskell, 2002b).

Increasing levels of urbanization and immigration and a shift to a knowledge-based economy requiring more highly skilled workers have intensified pressure on schools to reform the common schooling model. Pressure to reform this system of education has also come from marginalized and minority groups, who have contested the dominant ideologies implicit in and perpetuated by the common school movement. Based on the principles of equity and social justice, these groups have sought accommodations for their culture, identity, values, and beliefs. In a similar vein, parents seeking more voice in the socialization and education of their children have looked for schools more in line with their family values, child-rearing practices, and aspirations for their children. These social, political, and economic factors have created the impetus for ministries of education and school boards throughout Canada to consider alternative schooling arrangements (Gaskell & Levin, 2012; Manley-Casimir, 1982).

Proponents of school choice reforms argue that traditional public schooling, such as neighbourhood-based school assignments, governance by district, and a one-size-fits-all model of education, neglects the needs of diverse communities and individual learners and provides little incentive for schools to innovate and improve. Advocates herald school choice as a mechanism to encourage public schools to adopt leading educational practices to foster innovation in curriculum, instruction, and governance, as well as to introduce educational provisions to address the learning needs and interests of a diverse range of communities. By breaking the link between residence and school assignment, market forces are invoked that create competition among schools because parents now "vote with their feet" (Miron & Welner, 2012, p. 2), thereby creating incentives for schools to be more responsive to diverse parental interests and needs while also increasing student achievement outcomes. Advocates also argue school choice serves as a mechanism to promote greater equity and educational opportunity for all people and in particular for those students whose parents are unable to live in neighbourhoods with quality schools. Because neighbourhood schools can vary significantly in terms of quality and resources, advocates contend that school choice policies provide lower-income families with educational options they would not normally be able to access.

While proponents of school choice extol its virtues, opponents see the idea of educational markets as the commodification of education, which has traditionally been viewed as an essential public good and the great equalizer in terms of life chances for the most disadvantaged students. Critics raise concerns that school choice creates a multi-tiered public education system that perpetuates the segregation of students into increasingly unequal schools (Bosetti, 2005; T. Wilson, 2012). Opponents point to the fact that researchers have produced little compelling evidence indicating school choice programs increase student achievement or educational equity for underprivileged groups and argue that in some cases school choice policies can actually increase the problems they seek to ameliorate (D. Ball & Lund, 2010; Harrison & Kachur, 1999; A. Taylor, 2001a, 2001b). For example, sociologists (S. Ball, 2003; Ben-Porath, 2010; Bosetti, 2004; Bosetti & Pyryt, 2007; Power, Edwards, Whitty, & Wigfall, 2003) studying the impact of school choice on the reproduction of social class have concluded that school choice initiatives largely serve middle-class families who possess the appropriate social and cultural capital (time, education, resources) needed to navigate the process of successfully sending their children to their school of choice. As a result, students from disadvantaged backgrounds whose parents are not experienced in researching schooling options can be left behind in their neighbourhood schools. Because of a subsequent reduction in enrolment, these schools may find themselves grappling with decreased funding. Ultimately, opponents of school choice reject the idea that neoliberal-inspired[1] free market ideology should inform provisions for public education. Rather than creating an educational environment that pits school against school, where students inevitably compete with one another for admission to the best schools, opponents of school choice reform argue that policymakers should focus on ensuring that every neighbourhood has a quality school.

We see several limitations in how these school choice debates are often framed, both within the academic literature and within the greater public sphere. The first of these concerns the way normative assumptions regarding the aims and purposes of schooling are not always acknowledged by either detractors or advocates of school choice policies.

---

1 Neoliberalism comprises a set of political economic practices based on the proposition that human well-being is best advanced by "liberating individual entrepreneurial freedoms and skills within an institutional framework characterized by strong private property rights, free markets and free trade" (Harvey, 2009, p. 2).

Debates around school choice policies and their effects are difficult to resolve because they are ideologically based and philosophical in nature, reflecting fundamentally different beliefs and moral commitments regarding the aims and place of education within a democratic society. School choice provisions raise essential questions about "how individual rights are tempered by social obligations, how demands for liberty are balanced by demands for equality, and how private interests interact with public goods" (T. Wilson, 2012, p. 17). While conceptual debates regarding the merits of school choice will likely remain contentious, the need exists for a deeper understanding of the underlying theoretical and philosophical principles, aims, and context for which particular school choice policies are designed.

Through understanding the deeper philosophical principles that underlie particular school choice policies, it becomes possible to overcome the way debates are often framed as a dichotomous either/or proposition, where someone either is an unequivocal supporter of school choice or sees school choice as symbolic of the larger ills of market-based reforms. School choice policies can involve a range of possibilities that reside completely within the domain of the public education system, as well as private provisions of programs and services. Specific school choice policies have their advantages and their limitations, and should therefore be explored in a manner that avoids polemical arguments. Closely tied to this point is the problematic way discussions on school choice have been dominated by ideologically driven think tanks and interest groups that endorse free market reforms in education (Fraser Institute, Society for the Advancement of Excellence in Education, Canada West Foundation, C.D. Howe Institute). Reports commissioned by these sorts of groups tend to draw on selective empirical evidence to back their claims and ignore evidence or research that does not support their politically motivated arguments.[2] While these studies have argued that particular policies lead directly to positive educational outcomes, the empirical evidence suggests that the relationship between school choice and school improvement is much more complex and dependent on a

---

2 For example, the Fraser Institute's School Report Cards provide detailed tables on how well schools have performed in academics over a number of years in Alberta, British Columbia, Ontario, and Quebec. The Fraser Institute argues it provides this information so that parents can choose schools according to their academic performance and for teachers and administrators to identify areas of academic performance in their schools that need improvement: https://www.fraserinstitute.org/studies/school-report-cards.

variety of factors. These factors include how choice programs are designed; the conditions under which they are introduced; the subsequent actions that government, school systems, and educators take to implement them; and how families access school choice options (Lubienski, 2003, 2012; Ravitch, 2010; Smith, Wohlstetter, Farrell, & Nayfack, 2011).

Another problem with school choice debates concerns the way they often fail to attend to the unique context in which particular policies originated. Research focusing on one or two variables in a school choice plan, policy, or framework taken from a particular context does not immediately offer guidance on how another jurisdiction should proceed. For example, Michael Gove, education secretary of the Department for Education in the United Kingdom, gave a speech to the public policy exchange group regarding the benefits of further expanding British academy schools (Department for Education & Gove, 2011). In his speech, Gove made reference to the provisions of choice offered in the Albertan and Swedish Free School models and suggested the correlation is strong between the autonomous nature of these schools and their students' high levels of achievement. Yet in glossing over the particular educational contexts of Alberta and Sweden, he gave little consideration to the innumerable variables that contributed to these high levels of student achievement, including funding levels, innovative pedagogical practices, and demographic characteristics of student populations. In addition, he failed to explore other nuances present in these two contexts. For example, Alberta currently has only 15 charter schools that serve a small percentage of the province's total student population; therefore, little correlation can be made between the autonomy of these charter schools and the overall level of student achievement in Alberta.

While it can be argued that the contemporary school choice movement in Canada has largely been imported and adapted from American policies and frameworks, the aims and motivations for these policies have differed because of Canada's unique historical, sociocultural, and political context. For example, unlike in the United States, school choice in Canada is generally not hailed as a mechanism to boost test scores, promote the desegregation of students from minority groups, or improve failing inner-city schools. Provincial equalization policies in Canada lessen disparities between schools in different neighbourhoods or regions. Unlike the United States, Canada does not have a culture of high-stakes testing or standardized examinations for admission to universities (Davies & Aurini, 2008, p. 56). Moreover, Canadians generally rate their public schools more favourably than Americans do, which is bolstered by the fact that within key subject areas, Canadian students, unlike their American counterparts, consistently score near the top of the OECD's (Organisation for Economic Co-operation and Development) Programme for International Student Assessment (Brochu, Deussing, Houme, & Chuy, 2013).[3]

Debates around school choice in Canada are also unique because of specific rights and guarantees for francophone, anglophone, and Aboriginal peoples laid out in Canadian constitutional documents. For example, the Canadian Charter of Rights and Freedoms (Government of Canada, 2014a) guarantees francophone students outside Quebec the right to attend a francophone public school. Consequently, every provincial and territorial educational jurisdiction in Canada has a separate francophone board of education.

In light of various limitations to contemporary school choice debates, this book has a number of aims. To provide a broader context for how differing values give rise to different stances and sets of school choice policy options, we frame school choice controversies within broader philosophical debates. Our goal is to move beyond polemical debates about whether school choice is good or bad and towards how it can be conceived and implemented to complement and enhance public education in a democratic society. This final point requires that we step back and consider some of the underlying philosophical arguments about the rights of parents to decide the type of education their children receive, the permissible boundaries of educational provisions in a pluralist society, and the demands that a democratic society requires to ensure a level of stability and cohesion among its citizenry. We hope these discussions will provide a more nuanced understanding of whether particular school choice policies are appropriate within a given context.

Another aim of this book is to situate and examine school choice debates within the unique historical, political, and legal contexts of Canada. School choice debates in Canada stretch back to the very formation of the country and reflect negotiations by Canada's French-speaking populations to secure provisions to protect their unique cultural, religious, and

---

3 The Programme for International Student Assessment (PISA) is an international study launched by the OECD in 1997. It evaluates education systems worldwide every three years by assessing 15-year-olds' competencies in the key subjects of reading, mathematics, and science. To date, over 70 countries and economies have participated. Visit http://www.oecd.org/pisa/aboutpisa for details.

linguistic identity (Riffel, Levin, & Young,1996). In addressing the ways Canadian francophone people have significantly changed and shaped the contemporary school choice landscape, we see a need to outline how this situation was radically different for Aboriginal peoples (First Nations, Inuit, and Metis) who have historically been subject to a range of federal policies meant to eradicate their unique languages, cultures, and spiritual practices in an effort to assimilate them into the dominant Anglo-Canadian culture. Noting that educational options for parents of Aboriginal students are rarely addressed in the school choice literature, we summarize the steady increase of alternative provisions and educational autonomy that specifically seek to address the educational aims of Aboriginal peoples and communities.

Arguing that the use of school choice policies is on the rise in Canada, particularly in the west, we also highlight the degrees and variations of school choice options aimed at ethnic and religious minority groups, as well as alternative forms of schooling in various educational jurisdictions. Finally, to help inform which school choice models should guide policymaking decisions, we examine, where possible, the peer-reviewed research assessing the impact of particular school choice policies. We conclude this discussion by providing guiding principles for school districts to consider in deciding whether to approve or decline requests for specific school choice provisions.   Ideas for future use

Chapter Organization

We begin Chapter 1 by articulating three distinct philosophical arguments used for and against particular school choice policies: communitarianism, liberalism, and neoliberalism. In our discussion of liberalism, we attend to three strands within liberal theory: individual rights, equality of opportunity, and pluralism. These broader philosophical perspectives reflect differing moral commitments and understandings regarding the aims and purposes of public education. In identifying the major philosophical arguments used to critique or justify provisions for school choice, we explore criticisms levelled against each of these philosophical positions.

In Chapter 2, we consider the historical evolution of education in Canada in relation to national minority groups. We begin by outlining early constitutional negotiations that provided the French-speaking Quebecois with important provisions, including control over education, to preserve, protect, and promote their distinct francophone linguistic and religious identity. In the next section, we examine how this situation was radically different for Aboriginal national minority groups, who fought a long battle to gain control over how their children are educated. Highlighting recent federal policies that include some of these provisions, we outline a number of innovative programs across Canada that promote the unique languages, cultures, and spiritual practices of particular Aboriginal communities. We trace the emergence of Canada's official bilingualism policy, which gave francophones outside Quebec and anglophones in Quebec the constitutional right to have their children educated in French or English. We also note that this policy led to French immersion programs, which have become a very popular form of school choice for parents across Canada.

In Chapter 3, we turn to parallel calls by immigrant minority groups for greater recognition and accommodations for their distinct identities. We outline the ways in which the common school model of education sought to assimilate ethnic minority groups into the dominant Anglo-Canadian culture and English language. We discuss how the introduction of the Canadian Charter of Rights and Freedoms in 1982 (Government of Canada, 2014a), as well as the Canadian Multiculturalism Act in 1988 (Government of Canada, 2014b), provided a regulatory framework for integrating new arrivals into the larger Canadian society. We explore how various provincial educational jurisdictions have responded to these two legislative acts, including the extent to which religious minority groups have been able to secure public funding to establish faith-based and heritage-language schools. Noting Quebec's unique circumstances, we examine how Quebec has largely rejected the principles of multiculturalism and in its place has offered interculturalism as a framework for guiding school choice policies in the province.

In Chapter 4, we turn our attention to the historical evolution of educational reform movements that have shaped the contemporary school choice landscape in Canada. Our goal is to specifically outline the extent to which provincial and territorial educational jurisdictions allow for and provide funding to private, independent, and charter schools; for home-schooling; and for intra-district open enrolment.

In Chapter 5, we return to some of the concerns put forth by critics of school choice reform in Chapter 4 and examine the potential for these reforms to increase inequalities between socio-economic groups. We consider three concerns that commonly arise. First, the ways in which current school choice reforms rely on the ability of parents to access and negotiate available options. Second, parents' preferences about their children's education and social factors that influence parents' viewpoints may create biases that impede their decision on where to send their children to school. Third, school choice policies may create a hierarchy of subjects and disciplines that attract more families that are perceived as desirable to the detriment of marginalized groups.

In the final chapter, we provide a justification and rationale for school choice policies. We argue that the school choice debate must shift from supportive or oppositional ideological positions since it is historically embedded and will continue to be a fixture in public education. Instead, we need a focus on the evidence of the impact of these provisions for school choice on issues related to equity, social cohesion, and the enhancement of the quality of education for all students. As part of this argument, we defend the need for parents to have some discretion in making educational choices for their children, balanced with the larger collective, civic demands required of individuals in a democratic society. Finally, we conclude by providing guiding principles for policymakers and government officials in framing robust and egalitarian school choice policies.

Terminology of Various Canadian School Choice Programs

School choice policies range in their aims, mandates, and outcomes depending on how specific types of provisions are legislated and implemented. Public school choice options include charter schools, virtual schooling, open enrolment (intra-district), alternative programs, and magnet schools. In some provinces and territories, tax tuition credits subsidize private school tuition and provide public funds to support homeschooling. Private school choice is an option for parents who can pay the tuition and transportation fees for their children and meet the selective entrance requirement criteria to attend these schools.

We use the term *school choice* to refer to choice within the broad policy framework known as public education. *School choice* may be defined as the schemes that officially and directly give weight to parents' preferences regarding the allocation of their children to schools (McLaughlin, 2005). The term is culturally embedded and must be understood within appropriate social, political, and economic contexts. Depending on the historical period and political context, educators and policymakers have often used the term *school choice* to describe programs with limited commonality that may include language provision, alternative educational programs within public education, charter schools, and government funding for private schools. In the following paragraphs, we define terminology relevant to school choice options in Canada.

Public schools are tuition-free schools supported by taxes and controlled by a publically elected school board. These schools are open to all children in the provincially and territorially determined school jurisdiction. Typically, each school has a designated catchment zone to which students are assigned by the school board according to where they live.

Alternative schools, sometimes referred to as *magnet schools*, are public schools that offer special programs to attract parents and students throughout a school district. Such programs may be characterized by specialized curricular themes, philosophical predispositions, or instructional methods not available in mainstream schools within a particular school board's jurisdiction. They may operate as an alternative program within a neighbourhood school or as a stand-alone school. *Alternative schools* are often located in undersubscribed neighbourhood public schools.

Charter schools exist only in Alberta. Alberta Education (1996) defined charter schools as

> autonomous non-profit public schools designed to provide innovative or enhanced education programs that improve the acquisition of student skills, attitudes and knowledge in some measurable way ... [They] have characteristics that set them apart from other public schools in meeting the needs of a particular group of students through a specific program or teaching/learning approach while following Alberta Education's Program of Studies. (para. 1–2)

Teachers in charter schools may be associate members of the Alberta Teachers' Association. Charter schools are given considerable autonomy in governance and program delivery as long as they can demonstrate improved student learning and broaden the existing range of educational opportunities in the public school board. Unlike private schools, charter schools are non-denominational and cannot charge tuition fees or discriminate in student admission (Alberta Education, 2011a, p. 3).

Independent schools are private schools that charge tuition, allow for selective student admission policies, are governed by an elected or appointed board, and offer a variety of approaches in teaching, academic focus, and religious orientation (Clemens, Palacios, Loyer, & Fathers, 2014). Religiously affiliated independent schools in Canada are typically Catholic or Christian, with some provinces and territories having Islamic, Jewish, Mennonite, Amish, or Hutterite schools. Regulatory frameworks for independent schools vary among provinces and territories from heavy regulations in Quebec to no regulations in Ontario. Ministries of education that provide some funding to support independent schools require adherence to minimum requirements, such as following the provincially or territorially approved curriculum or program of studies. In some provinces and territories, criteria adherence serves as a form of accreditation, and unaccredited schools receive no funding.

Homeschooling is an option for all parents in Canada. Homeschooling is a form of instruction and learning that involves planned activities and takes place primarily at home in a family setting with a parent acting as the teacher or supervisor. Instruction may involve a tutor (Luke, 2003). All provinces and territories in Canada allow parents to educate their children at home[4] but require parents to notify a school board or an accredited private school of their intention. The school accepting the notification is responsible for monitoring the home education program and ensuring the children receive a reasonable education and meet compulsory school requirements.[5] Parents maintain primary responsibility for managing, delivering, and supervising their children's course of study, and the schooling authority monitors home education and student progress based on the program of study provided by the parents.

Online learning programs are educational programs offered by a school authority and delivered electronically to a student at a school site or off site under the instruction and supervision of a certified teacher of a board or accredited private school. Some parents choose to enrol their children in online learning programs to supplement home-based education or as an alternative to the parent-designed program of study. Online learning is not considered homeschooling if it supplements or supports compulsory education delivered in a school (Miron & Welner, 2012, p. 9).

Inter- and *intra-district choice* permits parents to "choose a public school other than the one assigned for their child or children within the district

---

4 Alberta is the only jurisdiction to provide funding for parents who school their children at home. Alberta gives $1641 per student annually and provides resources for parents. Given the option for all parents in Canada to homeschool their children, enrolment in homeschooling is low. For example, in Alberta, only 1.6% of students are homeschooled. Most provinces have enrolment rates below 0.5% (Clemens et al., 2014, p. 3).

5 All provincial Education Acts specify the ages between which students must attend school; this span varies, depending on the region, but is typically between 5 and 18 years of age. The Ministry of Education has the responsibility to ensure that students between these ages are receiving some form of schooling.

or in a surrounding district" (Miron & Welner, 2012, p. 10). Rules and restrictions usually apply, such as the preferred school having the space and support services to meet the needs of the child, particularly those with special learning needs, and parents covering the transportation costs. Intra-district is also referred to as *open enrolment policy*. However, in virtually all school districts students have a designated neighbourhood or catchment area school.

1

Philosophical Frameworks for Understanding School Choice in Canada

The controversies that surround school choice policies are underpinned by broader philosophical arguments that hinge on differing understandings of the fundamental purposes and aims of education. One reason for the difficulty in resolving these debates is that advocates and critics of school choice policies often use the same arguments to justify their positions. However, as T. Wilson (2012) noted, "The meanings of these terms vary across positions" (p. 17). For instance, school choice advocates may contend that particular school choice policies increase equity between schools and among families, giving families otherwise unable to afford alternative educational programs the opportunity to do so. Opponents similarly draw on the notion of equity to argue that school choice policies create positional advantages for middle-class families who have the time and resources to benefit from schooling options to the disadvantage of marginalized or lower-income families. While these two perspectives both use equity as a basis to advance their position, how they use this term is rooted in differing philosophical understandings of the aims of public education.

Before discussing the merits or lack thereof of specific school choice policies, a deeper appreciation of the philosophical justifications for and against school choice policies is necessary. In particular, it is important to understand how the concepts of "private" and "public" are central to these debates (T. Wilson, 2012). Examining the shifting political, cultural, and ideological terrain that informs what counts as public and private in relation to provisions for education raises fundamental questions concerning the degree to which schools can balance competing values linked to individual rights with broader social obligations, liberty rights with demands for social equality, and pluralistic conceptions of choice with a set of common societal values. While understanding how differing philosophical positions have responded to these core questions cannot resolve controversies around which framework should be used to guide educational policy within Canada, it can provide a basis for more informed and substantive debate and dialogue about school choice policies.

In this chapter, we outline three distinct philosophical arguments used for and against particular school choice policies: communitarianism, liberalism, and neoliberalism. These broad philosophical perspectives help elucidate differing moral commitments and understandings regarding the contested aims of public education. In identifying these central theoretical arguments, we explore critiques of each philosophical position. In our discussion of communitarianism, we note that school choice policies are generally framed in opposition to the "common school" ideal of a publicly funded, publicly governed school to which children are generally designated to attend based on where they live (T. Wilson, 2012, p. 19). We explore three strands within liberal theory – individual rights, equality of opportunity, and pluralism – that offer a philosophical basis for greater parental choice in deciding school type and location. We conclude this discussion with some of liberalism's limitations in relation to school choice and outline the neoliberal argument for school choice rooted in the economic theories of Friedman (1962). Given that this discourse has received a great deal of attention in contemporary school choice debates, we highlight various shortcomings of conceptualizing education in terms of a marketplace of options.

Communitarianism

Advocates of school choice policies in Canada stand in opposition to the traditional ideals of public education grounded in communitarianism. A core principle of communitarianism is that society needs to take the notion of promoting community seriously (Arthur, 2000). In taking community seriously, a basic ontological assumption exists that individuals are embedded within their communities through shared values, interests, and practices. The communitarian perspective criticizes atomistic notions of the self and suggests that individuals must be considered within their broader social contexts. Expressing this view, C. Taylor (1985) wrote, "Man is a social animal, indeed a political animal, because he is not self-sufficient alone, and in an important sense is not self-sufficient outside a polis" (p. 189). Individuals are not autonomous, isolated selves. They are necessarily connected to and embedded within communities. Within a communitarian framework, the premise that communities provide an inescapable and essential part of people's identity is not proposed as a voluntary or optional position but rather as a foundational element of what it means to be human. Daleney (1994) noted, "Communitarianism sees public life as a constitutive feature of human identity, and thus a necessary part of a good life and valuable for its own sake, not simply as an instrument for purely private ends" (p. 97). If one agrees with this premise, it is important to value the "communal dispositions that might unite people around a conception of what is good or worthwhile to pursue in life" (Arthur, 2000, p. 8).

Common good

Advocates of communitarianism generally stand against school choice policies based on an argument that such policies might erode the common good. Instead of a theory based on prioritizing rights that privilege the notion of the individual, the principles of communitarianism suggest a politics of a common good based on the notion that "individual citizens and voluntary groupings of individuals should make specific contributions to the common welfare of society" (Arthur, 2000, p. 81) is required. Two aspects are important to the notion of the common good. First is an implicit moral element taken up within Aristotelian notions of virtue and ethical values that need to be fostered among the citizenry (MacIntyre, 1984). Second is a political notion of the responsibilities that individuals owe to the broader society through communal dispositions (Etzioni, 1993). In the former, the common good becomes manifest in understanding the "good" of the individual in relation to the "good" of a community. The virtues for one person and for the community are the same. The good life is not interpreted as a private conception for the self but as particular habits of action cultivated for the broader good of society. For such theorists as Sandel (1998) and MacIntyre (1984), the common good involves a deep understanding of the moral values and commitments that imbue the actions of individuals as part of their membership within a political community, which is necessary to sustain a lifetime of moral fortitude and citizenship.

Common school

This overarching philosophical framework related to the individual's relationship to society leads to the promotion of the "common school model" (T. Wilson, 2012, p. 19) of education involving a district-run, publically governed school system that is free for students until the end of high school. Principles underpinning this compulsory public model of education reflect the ideal that schools should provide for children of different abilities, social, religious, and ethnic backgrounds. By creating an educational space that reflects the full diversity of society, children and adolescents can gain an appreciation and understanding of others while being enriched by the differences they encounter (Pring, 2008). However, in creating schools that reflect the diversity of society, another purpose is inherent to the common school model. Specifically, schools become a space to foster the common culture, language, and community that form the necessary foundation for ensuring that members of a diverse citizenry will be able to participate in the greater civic and democratic political community to which they belong. In this way, schools have a social and political purpose beyond learning; schools become instrumental in fostering a sense of social cohesion beyond the private domains of family and self. Informed by the principles of communitarianism, the common school model upholds the democratic ideals that many young nations were trying to foster in the early twentieth century. These ideals were based on the principle that schools should create a sense of social cohesion and stability while simultaneously promoting equality of opportunity and access for all.

While contemporary school choice policy debates are generally framed in opposition to traditional forms of public education embodied in this common school model, this model of public education is a relatively recent phenomenon. Until the early twentieth century, education often resided in the religious or private spheres. Educational models changed because of pressures from early-twentieth-century mass immigration to North America and the need to prepare a future workforce for increasingly expanding industrial enterprises (Friesen & Jardine, 2009). In light of this historical context, to more fully understand the principles that underpin the common school vision for education, it is necessary to understand how this model challenged two commonly held beliefs that had informed provisions for education up until the early twentieth century: (1) education is reserved for the elite, and (2) education is fundamentally a private good that should exist within private academies. The conception that schooling ought to be a public good, accessible and funded for all citizens, radically challenged previously held notions of schooling and its purposes.

Critique of communitarianism and the common school movement

While the notion of the common school became the dominant model for organizing education within developed liberal democracies throughout the twentieth century, this model has not been without its critics. One of the most prominent criticisms concerns how the common school model is focused primarily on creating a unitary vision of the nation-state, whereby a dominant national group uses its monopolistic power over what is taught in schools to privilege its own language, culture, history, and even in some cases, religion (Gereluk & Scott, 2014). Within the Canadian context outside Quebec, what became common, including the language of instruction and the perspective of the curriculum, reflected the values and culture of the Anglo-Canadian elite. Critics allege the common school model seeks to assimilate people from minority groups into the ethos of the dominant Anglo culture and English language. In trying to create this ideal of homogeneity through promoting a national common good, anyone who did not belong to the dominant national group was fundamentally excluded from or marginalized within the mainstream educational context.

As we explore in Chapter 2, Canada's French-speaking communities have historically contested an externally imposed common school model involving the imposition of British values on their society. Francophone communities have retained certain rights and governmental means to preserve and protect their distinct identity, and thereby developed a common school model of their own within Quebec. However, this has not been the case, until relatively recently, for Aboriginal peoples, who historically faced harsh and deeply destructive assimilatory education policies. As we explore in Chapter 3, provincial and territorial educational jurisdictions have sought to integrate various immigrant groups into the dominant English language and Anglo culture. For these groups, the common schooling model remained relatively uncontested until the 1960s and 1970s, when Aboriginal peoples and other minority groups increasingly contested exclusionary and assimilatory common schooling policies and instead advocated for new collective rights and multicultural policies and frameworks (Kymlicka, 2007, p. 61).

Liberalism

In light of criticisms surrounding who gets to define what is a "common good," a liberal framework offers a theoretical perspective that aims to better balance the competing demands of public and private interests within public education. Broadly speaking, the principles of liberal theory place a particular value on liberty, equality of opportunity, and tolerance for different ways of life (Rawls, 1999). Simply put, individuals have different ideas about how they want to lead their lives, particularly considering political, religious, and ideological differences. Given these competing doctrines, the liberal perspective affirms it is difficult – if not impossible – to come to public consensus about what constitutes a better or "good" life. Because of this impasse, liberalism recognizes a private sphere of life that respects individual choice related to ultimate goals, family life, occupation, and matters of personal taste. Liberalism places a heavy burden on the state to justify intervention in that area (Godwin & Kemerer, 2002, p. 67).

These private interests, however, are balanced within the broader public sphere of preserving individual liberties in a democratic society. The state is obligated to guarantee two higher-order interests for individuals: the interest of developing and exercising their capacity for a conception of "good," and the interest of developing and exercising a sense of justice (Rawls, 1999). The first of these interests seeks to ensure that individual benefits are protected within the larger society, while the second involves balancing liberty with equality so that one set of interests is not advantaged to the detriment of another. The philosophic foundations of liberalism require education to prepare students to make informed life decisions and to be active and engaged citizens, cultivating the democratic dispositions found in a pluralist liberal society. Liberalism is achieved by fostering both the personal autonomy and the civic responsibility necessary for a democracy. Inherent in school choice policy under a liberal framework is the articulation of the parameters of the authority of the state, professional educators (teachers), and parents in governing education and the upbringing of children. Within this overarching liberal framework, three philosophical notions frame contemporary school choice debates: individual rights and autonomy, equality of opportunity, and reasonable pluralism. We outline each of these and their implications for school choice policies.

Individual rights and autonomy

Many advocates of school choice policies draw on two tenets within liberalism to justify their position: the protection of individual rights and the need to foster autonomous individuals. Based on these principles, classical liberal philosophers, such as John Locke (1632–1704) and John Stuart Mill (1806–1873), argued for education to remain in the private sphere. For these theorists, state-provided and regulated schooling curtailed the fundamental aim of education, which was to foster autonomy and diversity in a liberal society (Gutmann, 1987). The constraints and uniformity found in state-regulated schools acted as tools of control and oppression rather than vehicles for freedom and choice. Locke and Mill viewed educational choice as a means to free the mind of prejudice and conformism. The role of the state, as they saw it, should be limited to providing funding for education, ensuring that the curriculum provided students with basic skills in numeracy and literacy. However, parents should oversee those elements of education related to conceptions of quality of life and character because they had the right to pass on their way of life to their children.

More recently, John Rawls's (1921–2002) central assumption, as we have noted, is that no groups in a society will ever agree on what constitutes the good life. He stated, "I should like to avoid, for example, claims to universal truth, or claims about the essential nature and identity of persons" (Rawls, 1985, p. 223). While Rawls was primarily interested in developing a political theory in response to a comprehensive notion of the "good," the principles of liberal theory have clear educational implications for developing school choice policies. One primary aim would be the emphasis on an education system where children develop the capacity to construct their own idea of the good life, as long as they do not jeopardize the rights of others, and have the freedom and authority to lead that good life. In this way, the overarching principle of autonomy in liberal theory has direct implications for an education system responsive to the various conceptions of what constitutes a good life. For this reason, Rawls's theory is commonly drawn on in considering the parameters of school choice policy (Brighouse, 2000; Gereluk, 2006; Reich, 2008).

If we start with the premise that one of the primary purposes of education is to foster autonomous individuals – specifically, individuals able to make informed judgments about how to lead their lives – then we might arguably distrust and be suspicious of what constitutes the "common good" and who gets to determine that. In this vein, Galston (1999) argued for an "expressive liberty" (p. 876) that supports a deference to parents' rights to choose how they lead their lives and raise their children, with minimal intervention from the state. From this stance, expressive liberty makes a clear distinction between the rights of the state and the rights of parents. Galston (1999) wrote:

> The state has the right to establish certain minimum standards, such as the duty of parents to educate their children, and to specify some minimum content of that education, wherever it may be conducted. Parents, however,

have a wide and protected range of choices as to how to discharge that duty
to educate. (p. 874)

Expressive liberty provides the ability to balance public and private
ideas, with a value placed on individuals' ability to foster their differing beliefs and values as individuals and within their associative groups.
Protecting a conception of the good under the principles of liberty and
autonomy necessitates that individuals should have access to distinctive
schools that allow for reasonable and varied conceptions of the good.
Accordingly, "individual rights to choose particular approaches to education are juxtaposed against a monolithic and mandatory system of education" (T. Wilson, 2012, p. 25).

Liberal theory offers a balance of the individual rights and liberties
that play out in school choice policies. We might suggest that, by itself,
liberal theory is not much different from a libertarian stance that has a
clear delineation between individual and state. At this point, liberal theorists consider the other key principles that balance out individual rights,
starting with the principle of equality of opportunity.

Equality of opportunity

One of the biggest debates in school choice policy is the principle of
educational equality. To understand the contested nature of how notions
of educational equality specifically play out in school choice debates,
we must first consider the fundamental value that "social and political
institutions should be designed or reformed to realize equal respect for
the value of all individual persons" (Brighouse, 2000, p. 116). Within this
overarching principle, Brighouse (2000) noted two facets of educational
equality creating two kinds of goods:

> [Educational equality] provides a competitive advantage in economies which
> distribute benefits and burdens unequally: being better educated enhances
> your prospective lifetime income and job satisfaction. It also provides non-
> competitive opportunities for fulfilling life experiences: not only the re-
> ward of executing excellently those tasks which demand the skills one has
> learned. (p. 116)

An argument in favour of promoting equality of opportunity specifically related to school choice is simply that wealthier families who can
move into better neighbourhoods with better quality schools, or who can

afford to pay for a higher quality of education, should not possess positional advantages over families who come from less advantaged circumstances. Rawls (1999) affirmed this notion of equality of opportunity, suggesting that

> those who are at the same level of talent and ability, and have the same willingness to use them, should have the same prospects of success regardless of their initial place in the social system, that is, irrespective of the income class in to which they are born. (p. 73)

School choice advocates suggest that when public school choice opportunities are limited, the middle class maintain the advantage: if they are unable to access their school of choice, they may have the resources to send their children to a private school or move into the neighbourhood in the catchment area for their school of choice. Creating school choice policies as an integral part of a public education system might mitigate this positional advantage by creating opportunities for disadvantaged families to have access to schools of their choice, rather than the one assigned to them based on the neighbourhood in which they live.

Having considered the principles of liberty and equality at the micro level, we turn to another key principle of liberal theory, reasonable pluralism, that considers how school choice policies might better reflect the diverse nature of democratic societies.

Reasonable pluralism

Parents engage a mixture of rationales in the selection of schools for their children. Their motivations are complex because ultimately public education requires them to surrender to the state some of their parental responsibility for the socialization and education of their children, which may entail their children being subjected to ideas that are inconsistent with their family values and beliefs. Within these parameters, parents are left to determine how best to preserve family values and traditions related to religion, culture, language, and identity; some choose specialized public or independent schools to support the socialization of their children, while others keep within their private sphere and choose to homeschool their children.

Given that the pluralist nature of society inherently involves a diversity of religious, political, and ethical approaches to life, a normative approach recognizes that the common school does not offer a morally neutral stance. Part of the problem with the common school ideal is that the historical record suggests public schools have demonstrated little respect for diversity of thinking among different political, religious, and ethical stances. Instead, public schools were found to "subjugate and coercively assimilate minority populations" (Reich, 2007, p. 715). School choice has the potential to make provisions for reasonable pluralism, particularly for students whose identity and self-understanding depend on the vitality of their own cultural, religious, ethnic, racial, or gender context. In contrast, the common school model can present potentially constraining elements and limit their prospects for living what they deem to be the good life (Gutmann, 1994). If the state seeks to prioritize the rights of the individual over the interests of the group, commonly referred to as *ethical individualism,* then the state must take the position that individual freedom and equality take priority over other aims (Reich, 2007).

Reich (2008) contended that school choice could be considered within the broader public parameters of pluralism in a society and provide a nice complementary balance:

> If we agree that one societal aim is to allow for pluralism, then it must necessarily adhere to the liberty principle in favour of school choice. Permitting parents to select a school for their children is crucial to respecting the liberty interests of parents. To be more specific, liberal societies must protect some version of school choice because the normative significance of pluralism requires the state to respect the liberty interests of parents to rear their children in some rough accordance with their deepest ethical or religious significance. (pp. 21–22)

Within this view, school choice provides a vehicle for promoting diversity within a broader pluralist society (Gaskell, 2002a). Critics suggest that such a view will create increased segregation and weaker notions of citizenship. However, Reich (2007) argued that distinctive schools can still uphold some of the broader norms of citizenship. School choice does not mean that citizens abandon a vision of the common aims of public education; rather, it advocates a balance between the diverse and varied private interests held in a pluralistic society and the broader civic aims required for a democratic society. In this way, these two principles do not exist within a false binary. Liberal theorists suggest that school choice may balance the values inherent in promoting reasonable pluralism with the broader civic purposes of public education (Gutmann, 1987; Reich, 2007).

well as by their potentially limited understanding of the learning needs and interests of their children. They require sufficient social and cultural capital, resources, time, and connections to effectively participate in "choice work," which involves gathering and interpreting information, engaging in conversations with teachers and school administration, and filling out the appropriate forms to have their children admitted to the school of their choice (Andre-Bechely, 2005).

One of the strongest criticisms of the proliferation of school choice policies is that it exacerbates the positional advantages of middle-class families who already have better educational prospects for their children because "higher earnings enable families to enrich the learning environments in which their children develop" (Duncan & Murname, 2011, p. 19). While this middle-class advantage is prevalent regardless of school choice policies, the economic divide is widened when school choice policies are incorporated within a public education system that cannot attend to the hidden costs or supplemental fees that may limit the opportunities of lower-income families to engage in such programs. Transportation to and from school; extra costs for uniforms, extracurricular activities, or field trips; and supplemental tutoring all represent expenses that some parents may simply not be able to afford (S. Ball, 2007). Critics fear that school choice policies may lead to an elitist, two-tiered school system that separates the "haves" and the "have nots" (Barlow & Robertson, 1994; A. Taylor, 2001b).

Critics of school choice argue that educational markets respond to the self-interests of parents as consumers and that choice options undermine the principle of equality of opportunity in the sense that educational outcomes will be influenced by the wealth and preferences of parents, rather than the abilities and efforts of students. S. Ball (2003) described parental choice as a "middle-class" strategy that reproduces that group's relative social class advantage and secures opportunities for their children's social advancement and mobility. Children from families not in the position to play the educational market to their benefit are disadvantaged.

Lareau (2002) argued these advantages emerge from values inherent in what she termed *concerted cultivation* (p. 748), an intensive form of parenting in which "middle-class parents increasingly structure their children's lives and treat them as projects-in-the-making [and] ... align their child-rearing practices with school requirements," (Davies & Aurini, 2008, p. 55) altering their relationships with public educators from "mere supportive roles to more directing and even adversarial roles" (Davies & Aurini, 2008, p. 55). For Canadian parents, choice seeking and intensive forms of parenting (i.e., concerted cultivation) are nuanced activities reflecting strong irrational qualities of moral, expressive dimensions rooted in "parents' sense of their children's worth, individuality and self-actualization" (Davies & Aurini, 2008, p. 68). Among those who engage in this form of parenting, actively selecting the appropriate school for their children is an expression of responsible parenting.

If part of the reality of school choice policies is that some parents will create positional advantages for their children to the disadvantage of others, then this process undermines the broader principles of liberal theory. For principles of liberalism to remain viable, individual rights must be balanced with equality of opportunity, specifically in relation to protecting the most disadvantaged members of society. We now turn to the final section where we look to the most common theoretical perspective that has informed recent school choice policies – that of neoliberalism.

Neoliberalism

Much of the neoliberal theory that has held a prominent position within education reform movements, particularly since the 1980s, is largely attributable to the contributions of economist Milton Friedman in his 1962 publication, *Capitalism and Freedom*. Friedman made the important distinction between financing and governing public schools, arguing that the two are distinct notions and must be treated separately. He challenged that while government may be charged with funding public schools, it does not necessarily follow that it should be charged with governing public schools. In defence of this proposition, Friedman conceptualized the notion of vouchers, which would allow the funding to follow the student, rather than funding being allocated to the school. He wrote:

> The desirability of such nationalization has rarely been faced explicitly. Governments have, in the main, financed schools by paying directly the costs of running educational institutions. Thus this step seemed required by the decision to subsidize schooling. Yet, the two steps could readily be separated. Governments could require a minimum level of schooling financed by giving parents vouchers redeemable for a specified maximum sum per child if spent on "approved" educational services. (Friedman, 1962, p. 89)

Based on laissez-faire free market principles, Friedman's (1962) early conceptions of lessening the state's role in public schooling provided the theoretical basis for challenging the provision of public schools. Advocates of school choice policies based on Friedman's conceptualization argue choice can enhance parental freedom and parents' control over their children's education and, from a social perspective, improve the quality of schools and provide equal access to quality schooling. The logic of these assertions is based on the belief that stimulating market forces in education will provide incentives for schools to raise their performance because parents prefer schools that are pedagogically effective. Providing parents with information regarding school performance and granting them discretion to choose a school will channel demand towards effective schools.

While making these claims, individuals on the political right assert that the spirit of competition and excellence have been sacrificed to make the educational system conform to socialist notions of social justice, resulting in a system that promotes mediocrity over merit and standards of excellence (P. Brown, 1997). They call for the injection of educational market principles as a way to revitalize public education by creating public and private alternatives, thereby fostering competition among schools for student enrolment. This change would make schools more responsive to the needs and interests of parents and students, and enhance productivity and efficiency. In this way, competition for students encourages schools to improve their approaches to instruction, devise entrepreneurial strategies to be more cost-effective, and differentiate their curriculum in ways that improve the academic quality of the school. Advocates of this position argue the combined effect of these efforts leads to an aggregate increase in student achievement (Belfield & Levin, 2002; Chubb & Moe, 1990; Davies & Aurini, 2011).

Tension is inherent between accountability–quality assurance reform strategies and market-based choice reforms, though these often go hand in hand within policy frameworks that focus on structural educational reform. Quality assurance strategies serve to centralize governance and decision making regarding curriculum mandates, standardized testing, and fund allocation. In contrast, choice reform frameworks are premised on the necessity of decentralizing power by stimulating markets in ways that empower parents and teachers (Forsey et al., 2008).

This tension plays out in how school choice policy is designed and implemented and what level of state control is used in directing educational markets. For example, government policy sets the parameters to create the conditions (structures, processes, and regulations) necessary for educational markets to function as a competitive marketplace by using such mechanisms as vouchers, tuition credits, and charter schools. The state, rather than unfettered markets, maintains control of education through funding formulas and accountability schemes to monitor efficiency, as well as through core curriculum and standardized testing that monitors student achievement and institutional effectiveness. In contrast, neoliberal market-based school choice policies seek to transfer the responsibility for the provision of programs and services to the school board and individual schools, wherein parents would provide the metric for quality provision of schooling by voting with their feet. The market-based philosophy maintains that good schools will attract parents, and mediocre schools will become undersubscribed and ultimately shut down.

The criticisms of neoliberalism and school choice policies involve a deep scepticism that market-based policies create a greater variety and better quality of schools. Specifically, neoliberalism assumes individuals make informed, rational choices about the various school choice provisions; competitive market mechanisms create more efficiencies and a higher quality of schooling; and market mechanisms do not undermine other educational values through a privileging of particular forms of knowledge. In the previous section we noted the limits of rational choice theory, so let us consider these last two criticisms of school choice policies based on the principles of neoliberalism.

One of the main criticisms is that market-based mechanisms are an inappropriate metric to apply to the public institution of schools. Broadly speaking, neoliberal theorists tend to take an overly pessimistic view of the role of the state and, conversely, may have an overly optimistic view of the market (Brighouse, 2004). Brighouse (2004) has noted that simply relying on competition among parents to choose well to ensure better quality schooling does not take into consideration schools located in more vulnerable geographic areas (high-poverty areas, areas with gangs, ghettos) to which parents might feel less comfortable sending their children. Neoliberal theorists in education rely on the assumption that market-based principles can improve education in those more diverse and challenging areas. Sceptics suggest the nature of public educational institutions is more complex, and market mechanisms will not necessarily attract parents to schools or areas that have more challenging circumstances. For instance, relying on market mechanisms does not consider how to provide a quality education in schools located where the population is low, where crime is high, or where students' needs may be disproportionately more costly to serve (such as for recent immigrants or refugees).

Yet more troubling, note critics of neoliberal theory, is that neoliberal theory repositions the role of public education and arguably diminishes the democratic ideals of public education in two ways. First, school choice may create homogenous student populations that are unreflective of the larger society. School choice policies segregate children through the creation of value communities that reflect "little fiefdoms" catering to the needs, values, and interests of particular groups (Bosetti, 1998b, 2000; Gewirtz, Ball, & Bowe, 1995; Whitty, Power, & Halpin, 1998). In creating more homogenous student populations that attract like-minded families to a school marketing a specific educational mandate, students are segregated into narrowly defined communities. Students who attend an alternative school that targets a particular kind of student and family have limited exposure to students from different backgrounds. Likewise, students who remain in mainstream schools lose exposure to students who leave in favour of the alternative option (Gereluk, 2006). As a result, specialized schools with programs of choice have the potential to Balkanize students into closed school communities, thereby undermining the fostering of democratic ideals in public education.

Second, critics contend that school choice policies shift authority and responsibility to control and direct education policy away from elected state authority and into the hands of market mechanisms (Molnar, 1996; Ranson, 1993). This greater concern regarding the infusion of choice mechanisms into the public education system centres on the problematic ways that market mechanisms, rather than democratic debate, determine the goals and values of education. Market solutions commodify education, in effect privatizing the public good. Parents are positioned as consumers with the responsibility of exercising choice, either actively by seeking a particular school or passively by sending their children to their neighbourhood school.

Conclusion

Education policy has oscillated among competing goals, ranging from egalitarian concerns (equal access to education), to efficiency and effectiveness (fiscal responsibility and accountability for student achievement), to individual concerns (freedom of choice), and to concerns for social justice (rights of the disadvantaged, urban poor, and minority groups). Expressing the goals of education in terms of democracy and the common good underscores citizens' collective interest in education and their shared responsibility in the development of future generations. Placing education into the private sphere emphasizes the importance of education in providing opportunities for self-realization and the development of personal and group autonomy.

The state wields considerable authority in the construction of educational school choice policies. While a principled commitment to freedom is a core value of democracy, in framing and communicating the various options parents have in public school choice, policymakers need to take into consideration more directly the challenges and limitations of parents and families in exercising choice. Policymakers have a responsibility to ensure the mechanisms are in place to control choice through sufficient regulations, financial support, and services, such as access to information about programs offered, school choice counselling for families, and programs that address the needs of the most disadvantaged, to ensure parents can exercise choice on a level playing field. For school choice policy to fulfil its promise of enhancing the quality of education for all children and of advancing the goals of equality and freedom, governments need to focus not only on providing for choice and choice sets but also on enabling families and individuals to exercise choice to realize the benefits of meeting their children's learning and developmental needs.

2

Educational Accommodations
for National Minority Groups

WRITTEN WITH DAVID SCOTT

In this chapter we examine the historical and constitutional foundations for the provision of school choice in Canada in relation to regionally concentrated national minority populations. According to Kymlicka (1998), national minority groups can be distinguished from immigrant minority groups who came to the country by choice; a national minority group constitutes a "historical society, with its own language, and institutions, whose territory has been incorporated (often involuntarily, as is the case with Quebec) into a larger country" (p. 2). Within Canada, national minority groups are Aboriginal peoples (i.e., First Nations, Metis, and the Inuit) and the Quebecois (the biggest French-speaking population in Canada). Unlike immigrant minority groups in Canada, Aboriginal peoples and the Quebecois have demanded the right to govern themselves in areas including education (Kymlicka, 1998, p. 6). As a result of both historic and contemporary negotiations, national minority groups in Canada have secured varying degrees of autonomy and control over their children's education. In this way, national minority groups have significantly changed and shaped the school choice landscape in Canada.

In addressing how the school choice landscape has been affected by educational provisions for national minority groups in Canada, we specifically explore how the provinces and territories, and in the case of Aboriginal peoples, the federal government, have negotiated and amended their educational policies in light of key federal legislation, including the Constitution Act (1867), the Indian Act (1876), the Official Languages Act (1969), and the Canadian Charter of Rights and Freedoms (1982). This chapter consists of three sections. We begin with an outline of early constitutional negotiations that granted the French-speaking Quebecois important provisions, including control over education, to preserve, protect, and promote their distinct francophone identity. We consider stipulations within these agreements that protect the religious rights of Protestants in Quebec and Roman Catholics in some provinces and territories outside Quebec.

In the second section, we examine how this situation was radically different for Aboriginal national communities, who have historically been subject to a range of federal policies meant to eradicate their unique languages, cultures, and spiritual practices in an effort to assimilate them into the dominant Anglo-Canadian culture. We explore how, since the early 1970s, Aboriginal peoples and communities have fought to gain control over how their children are educated. Noting the introduction of recent federal policies that include some of these provisions, we highlight a number of innovative programs across Canada that offer educational spaces that promote the unique languages, cultures, and spiritual practices of particular Aboriginal communities. In the third section, we trace the emergence of Canada's official bilingualism policy, which gave francophone people outside Quebec and anglophones in Quebec the constitutional right to have their children educated in their respective language. We document the rise of French immersion programs across Canada, which have their roots in Canada's official bilingualism policy.

The Constitution Act of 1867:
Religious Rights for Catholics and Protestants

The first forms of school choice policies in Canada emerged out of negotiations during the Charlottetown Conference of 1864 among representatives from the colonies of British North America discussing their possible union as a Canadian Confederation. One of the central considerations during these negotiations concerned demands by both French and British colonialists to create a federal structure and set of constitutional arrangements that would ensure they could each preserve their cultural heritage and identity expressed through language (French and English) and religion (Roman Catholic and Protestant). When the Dominion of Canada was formed in 1867, a number of measures were included in the Constitution Act (originally called the British North America Act) to address these demands (Government of Canada, 2014c). The first of these measures included creating a federal structure where the United Province of Canada was divided into the provinces of Quebec and Ontario so that anglophones would have a demographic majority in Ontario and the Quebecois would have a majority in Quebec. As part of this new federal framework, many powers were devolved to the provincial level, providing the Quebecois control over areas central for maintaining their unique identity, including language, religion, and education.

As a result of these measures, Section 93 of the Constitution Act gave exclusive control over education to each government at the provincial level (Government of Canada, 2014c). However, to protect the minority religious rights of Protestants in Quebec and Roman Catholics in Ontario, Section 93 guaranteed the delegation of these powers to the provincial level on the condition that

> (1) Nothing in any such Law shall prejudicially affect any Right or Privilege with respect to Denominational Schools which any Class of Persons have by Law in the Province at the Union;
>
> (2) All the Powers, Privileges, and Duties at the Union by Law confined and imposed in Upper Canada on the Separate Schools and School Trustees of the Queen's Roman Catholic Subjects shall be and the same are hereby extended to the Dissentient Schools of the Queen's Protestant and Roman Catholic Subjects in Québec. (Government of Canada, 2014c, Section 93, para. 1–2)

These provisions ensured that Catholics outside Quebec, and Protestants inside Quebec, retained the right to have their own schools. These schools, moreover, had to be fully funded by the provincial government and run by a separate and autonomous school board made up of members drawn from within the religious community. By preserving the unique denominational character of public education that existed in Canada before Confederation, the foundation was laid for two distinct publicly funded education systems: one secular with a historically Protestant ethos, and the other Roman Catholic with a historically Catholic ethos.

Beyond Ontario, these provisions have since specifically affected the provinces of Alberta, Saskatchewan, and Newfoundland, which, after joining the Canadian confederation, introduced fully funded Catholic school boards. Notably, however, in 1997 Newfoundland amalgamated its Catholic school system into the secular public system. Statistically, enrolment in these schools varies, with 21.1% of the total student population attending a Catholic school in Saskatchewan, while 30.3% of the total student population attends a Catholic school in Ontario (Clemens et al., 2014). In Quebec, anglophones were served by a parallel Protestant school system until 1993. Since then, children who can prove at least one parent is an anglophone can attend a school within an English school board. In all of Canada, only Alberta, Saskatchewan, and Ontario have fully funded Protestant or Catholic separate school boards.

The early constitutional agreements that occurred during Canada's formation as a country are significant for the evolution of school choice policies into the present in two important respects. First, because of these arrangements, the 10 provinces and three territories that now make up the Canadian federation each has its own Ministry of Education and is not subject to any federal oversight. Therefore, each province and territory has responded to the demands of school choice reform in diverse ways. Second, because of the historical provisions for the accommodation of English and French minority religious rights, school choice policies have been part of the Canadian educational landscape in significant ways.

From Assimilation to Increasing Autonomy: The Case of First Nations Education

Despite legal requirements defined in the Constitution Act of 1867 to ensure religious rights for minority Roman Catholic or Protestant populations, the act provided no parallel rights for Aboriginal peoples of Canada or their diverse languages, cultures, and traditions. This absence was particularly noticeable in light of the existence of Aboriginal peoples as distinct national communities long before the formation of the Canadian state and the significant contributions they made to Canada's political and economic formation. From a political point of view, this included Aboriginal leaders signing treaty agreements with both the British Crown and the Canadian government, which allowed for European settlement on their traditional territories. In the case of treaty agreements negotiated in the late nineteenth century across the plains, Aboriginal leaders sought to ensure that provisions for education were included in these agreements in the hope that this would aid their communities in adjusting to the new economic, social, and political realities they were facing (Royal Commission on Aboriginal Peoples, 1996, p. 134).

However, once the Canadian government had secured these lands for settlement, under section 91(24) of the Constitution Act, federal policymakers quickly enacted the Indian Act of 1876 with the aim of consolidating all previous legislation targeted towards First Nations peoples. Within the Indian Act, First Nations peoples' rights were limited to Status Indians, while the rights of Inuit, Metis, and non-status Indians were relegated to provincial or territorial responsibility. Ironically, despite the fact that First Nations leaders had negotiated treaty agreements to ensure they maintained parts of their traditional territory, the Indian Act would ultimately name these lands *reserves*, defined as a tract of land set aside for the exclusive use of Indian bands (University of British Columbia, First Nations Studies Program, 2009).

The Indian Act (Canadiana, 2015) severely limited what First Nations would be allowed to do, including their autonomy over their children's education. Sections 114 to 122 of the Indian Act authorized the Minister of Indian and Northern Affairs to enter into agreements with religious or charitable organizations, public or separate school boards, and the provinces and territories to provide schooling for on-reserve First Nations children. The act made no reference to substantive issues regarding curriculum content or provisions that would help ensure the quality of education in these schools. However, sections 120 to 121 permitted Protestants or Roman Catholics of any band to have separate faith-based day schools or day school classes on the reserve (if numbers warranted). This section also stipulated that teachers had to be from the respective Protestant or Roman Catholic denomination. Notably, the act did not provide the Minister of Indian Affairs the legal right to enter into agreements with First Nations councils to operate their own schools. As a result, historically it has been the prerogative of the minister, not parents, to designate the school First Nations children should attend.

Unlike the religious autonomy given to the French Roman Catholic and English Protestant settlers, virtually no self-governing powers were given to Aboriginal peoples who, in contrast, faced severe and harsh assimilation policies. These policies sought to have Aboriginal peoples give up their identity, shift their allegiance to the British Empire and Canadian government, and adopt anglophone, and in some cases francophone, values. As outlined in the Indian Act, the core purpose of the federal government's educational policies towards Aboriginal peoples was to provide

> the legal basis for the internment of Aboriginal children and to establish government control as a means of pursuing assimilation of these children into majority white Euro-centric culture, and effectively eliminate the influence of aboriginal traditional knowledge or culture on the development of these children. (Mendelson, 2008, p. 3)

With this "civilizing" aim in mind, beginning in the 1870s the Indian Act provided the legal basis for the forcible removal and internment of Aboriginal children into mainly Protestant- and Catholic-run industrial schools (later called residential schools). Built on the "assumption that Aboriginal cultural and traditions were inferior and unequal," the ultimate aim of residential schools was to "kill the Indian in the child" (Aboriginal Affairs and Northern Development Canada, 2008b, para. 2).

During the twentieth century, 130 residential schools were introduced in every territory and province except Newfoundland, Prince Edward Island, and New Brunswick. The last residential school did not close until 1996 (Truth and Reconciliation Commission of Canada, 2012). The Truth and Reconciliation Commission of Canada (2012) reported that over 150,000 Aboriginal, Inuit, and Metis children were sent to residential schools, where they were prohibited from seeing their families, speaking their first languages, or practising their traditional cultural teachings. The commission has also documented the ways in which children were often harshly disciplined; insufficiently fed, clothed, and housed; and victim to various forms of emotional, physical, and sexual abuse. The commission has estimated that over 80,000 former residential students are still alive today, many of whom continue to experience deep emotional trauma because of the treatment they received while attending a residential school. This lasting damage has led to what the commission refers to as a "lost generation" of people who lack a sense of self-worth and connection to their Aboriginal language and culture because of how their Aboriginal identity was devalued within these schools. The legacy of the residential school system has had a profoundly negative impact on Aboriginal communities and people and has contributed to many of the social problems in Aboriginal communities today (Fontaine, 2010; Regan, 2010).

As would be expected, these policies prompted deep political resistance on the part of Aboriginal peoples, who pressed for self-governance and control over the education of their children. In 1972, this resistance coalesced into the formation of the National Indian Brotherhood (the precursor to the Assembly of First Nations), which went on to publish the policy paper *First Nations Control of First Nations Education* (Assembly of First Nations, 2010). Similar to Quebecois' demands for measures to ensure the preservation of their language and culture, the National Indian Brotherhood saw education as crucial to ensuring the survival and continuation of Aboriginal traditions, languages, and spiritual practices. As a result, this policy document demanded that Aboriginal peoples and communities be given autonomy and control in education so they could create a vision for education that would align with their unique cultural identity. The document stated:

We want education to provide the setting in which our children can develop the fundamental attitudes and values which have an honored place
in Indian tradition and culture ... We believe that if an Indian child is fully
aware of the important Indian values he will have reason to be proud of
our race and of himself as an Indian. (Assembly of First Nations, 2010, p. 1)

Because Aboriginal peoples were excluded in the historical processes
of creating public institutions for the education of their children and
were, moreover, subject to profoundly destructive assimilatory policies,
in outlining this vision for education, the National Indian Brotherhood
was seeking a new relationship with the federal government whereby
they could work to counter this historical wrong.

Beginning in 1974, Minister of Indian Affairs Jean Chrétien took steps
to put partial control of education back in the hands of First Nations
people and communities (Assembly of First Nations, 2010). From that
time forward, the federal government began funding both Aboriginal
students who chose to go to school off reserve and the band councils and
other First Nations educational authorities that operated their own on-
reserve schools. As a result, band-run schools have been able to hire more
Aboriginal teachers and staff – often from within the community – and introduce language classes and curricular initiatives that reflect the culture
and traditions of their nation. But even with these changes, as outlined
in the Indian Act, on-reserve schools continue to exist under the sole authority of the federal government. Moreover, on-reserve schools receive
only 75% of the per-student funding allowed for non-Aboriginal students
who attend provincially and territorially run schools (Bell et al., 2004).

Today in Canada, there are 520 band-operated schools and seven federal schools (six in Ontario and one in Alberta; National Panel on First
Nation Elementary and Secondary School Education for Students on
Reserve, 2011). According to the Chiefs Assembly on Education (2012,
p. 2), in 2010, more than 109,000 First Nations students resided on reserve lands. About 60% of these students attended on-reserve schools operated by First Nations band councils, 40% attended off-reserve schools
under provincial and territorial authority, and a few thousand attended
private schools (Mendelson, 2008). Approximately 75% of students who
attend an on-reserve elementary school transfer to an off-reserve school
to complete their secondary education (Chiefs Assembly on Education,
2012, p. 2).

Some of the primary goals of Aboriginal education have involved attempts to create educational spaces dedicated to providing culturally

appropriate education, preserving Aboriginal languages, and ensuring that Aboriginal Elders and community members are involved in the learning process. Educational authorities and Aboriginal communities have responded to these aims in a variety of ways. One of the most notable examples is the Mi'kmaw Kina'matnewey Education Authority created in 1999 through a partnership among the Mi'kmaq Nation, the federal government, and the Nova Scotia provincial government. The Mi'kmaw Kina'matnewey Educational Authority, which acts as a school board for 11 of the 13 Mi'kmaw communities in Nova Scotia, is the only Aboriginal school authority in Canada that operates under its own Education Act (Schwartz, 2013). According to the 2013 *Mi'kmaw Kina'matnewey Annual Report*, this educational authority has been tremendously successful (Schwartz, 2013). In 2007, 88% of its students graduated from high school, slightly higher than the number for non-Aboriginal Canadians (Schwartz, 2013, Mi'kmaq Education Act section, para. 6). These findings are confirmed by the Assembly of First Nations (2012, p. 2), which noted this percentage has gone up in some communities, including the Membertou First Nation, which achieved 100% graduation rates in the years before 2012.

Another notable example of Aboriginal peoples gaining control and autonomy in education involves the formation of Nunavut, which separated from the Northwest Territories in 1999. Similar to Quebec, Nunavut was created to provide the Inuit people with a political territory where they would form the majority of the population. In 2009, Inuit leaders introduced a new Education Act with the goal of ensuring that all students from kindergarten to grade 3 receive a bilingual education in a language such as Inuktitut or Inuinnaqtun and in English ("Nunavut Struggles," 2011). Although this aim has been reached in some schools, the territory has struggled to achieve this goal in all schools because of a lack of qualified teachers fluent in an Inuit language.

Beyond creating a separate school authority or political unit to give Aboriginal peoples control over education, several on-reserve band-run schools have successfully created educational spaces that support traditional cultural practices and languages while also preparing students to become successful participants in the larger Canadian economy and society. One of these is the Chief Atahm Elementary School on the Adams Lake Reserve in British Columbia (T'selcéwtqen Clleqmél'ten, 2013). In this elementary school, teachers do not instruct in English until grade 4, and teachers and parents, rather than the Ministry of Education, create the curriculum (Hyslop, 2011b). Through providing instruction in the

Secwepemctsin language, Chief Atahm Elementary School offers one of the few Aboriginal full immersion school programs in Canada.

Alongside educational innovations within band-run schools on reserves, Aboriginal parents and communities have partnered with public school districts to introduce schools that seek to be more culturally sensitive and responsive to Aboriginal students, cultures, and world views. Public school boards with large numbers of First Nations students often have Aboriginal advisory councils and consult with First Nations representatives in decisions related to accommodation of Aboriginal learners (Mendelson, 2008, p. 4). However, some school boards have gone further, introducing schools dedicated to Aboriginal students. For example, the Edmonton Public School Board created the Amiskwaciy Academy for grades 7 to 12, which strives "to honour the Aboriginal community and reflect its cultures, values, ancestral knowledge and traditions in achieving excellence in education" (Amiskwaciy Academy, n.d., para. 1). While Amiskwaciy Academy was the first of its kind in Canada, other school boards have promised to introduce similar schools. For instance, the Vancouver School Board has recently proposed opening the Vancouver Aboriginal School, which would adopt "the district's much-lauded Aboriginal Education Enhancement Agreement with local First Nations. Students would be taught by Aboriginal and Aboriginal-aware teachers, and involve parents, elders and community in the decision-making process" (Hyslop, 2011a, p. 1). In 2003, Alberta Education approved Mother Earth's Children's Charter School for students from kindergarten to grade 9; it became the first provincially recognized Indigenous charter school in Canada.

Despite these positive developments, many Aboriginal students, both on and off reserve, are struggling within the constraints of formal school settings. Approximately 60% of First Nations on-reserve residents ages 20 to 24 have not completed high school or obtained an alternative diploma or certificate (Statistics Canada, 2006, p. 19). In comparison, 87% of non-Aboriginal people in Canada in this demographic have completed high school. Studies have additionally found significant disparities in academic achievement levels between Aboriginal and non-Aboriginal students. Aboriginal students in British Columbia, for instance, make up more than 38% of the students in lower academic alternative programs in provincially run schools, while composing only 11% of the overall student body (British Columbia Ministry of Education, 2013, p. 7). According to some studies, lack of attendance is cited as one of the most significant reasons that Aboriginal students are failing to continue in their studies (Bell et al., 2004; Madvor, 1995). Many policy leaders attribute the challenges Aboriginal students are having in contemporary school settings to the legacies of the residential school system that continue to live in powerful ways within their communities. In addition, they point to the racism many Aboriginal youth experience within formal systems of education, which is reflected not only in their interactions with other students but also in the ways "Aboriginal values, perspectives and cultures are marginalized or nonexistent in the curriculum and the life of the institution" (Royal Commission on Aboriginal Peoples, 1996, p. 405).

In 2008, the Government of Canada formalized its commitment to reforming First Nations education and improving education outcomes for First Nations students in band-operated and provincial and territorial schools (Aboriginal Affairs and Northern Development Canada, 2012). In addition to partnerships already established in British Columbia and Nova Scotia, the federal government signed education agreements with Aboriginal and provincial educational authorities in Quebec, Prince Edward Island, Alberta, Manitoba, and New Brunswick, as well as with the Saskatoon Tribal Council (Aboriginal Affairs and Northern Development Canada, 2008a). While the nature of these agreements varied based on the terms negotiated with specific Aboriginal communities in each province, the *Memorandum of Understanding for First Nations Education in Alberta* (Government of Canada, 2010) reflects many of the key principles common to these various agreements:

1 Work collaboratively and expeditiously to continuously improve educational outcomes for First Nation students;

2 Recognize the diversity of First Nation peoples, communities, language, culture, traditions, and spiritual practices, and the need for standards-based and culturally appropriate education;

3 Ensure First Nation students have equitable access to quality education and smooth transitions between First Nation and provincial schools;

4 Achieve comparable quality and standards between First Nation on-reserve and provincial education;

5 Enhance governance, policy, program, and fiscal accountability to students, communities, and funding agencies;

6 Empower and engage First Nation elders, students, parents, and communities to improve educational outcomes;

7 Maximize effectiveness of existing activities and investments, and pursue initiatives to improve educational outcomes; and

8 Promote building of institutional capacity and relationships. (p. 3)

Paralleling these developments, in 2008, Prime Minister Stephen Harper, on behalf of the federal government, issued a statement of apology to former students of residential schools. In this speech, he made a commitment to forge a new relationship

> based on the knowledge of our shared history, a respect for each other and a desire to move forward together with a renewed understanding that strong families, strong communities and vibrant cultures and traditions will contribute to a stronger Canada for all of us. (Aboriginal Affairs and Northern Development Canada, 2008b, para. 12)

In light of the government's stated commitment to reconciliation, the Assembly of First Nations (2010) released *First Nations Control of First Nations Education*, calling for the "right and responsibility to exercise free, prior and informed consent in all education decisions that affect First Nations citizens, regardless of place of residence or type of institution" (p. 6). The document further advocates for the creation of a comprehensive First Nations education system that would lead to the cultural restoration and preservation of Aboriginal languages, knowledge, and cultures, while also affirming the value and role of Aboriginal traditions and cultures for living in modern times. To achieve these ends, the authors of this document challenged the federal government to adequately fund a system of education founded on a lifelong learning model, where the collective rights of Aboriginal peoples for autonomy and self-determination for their children's education are recognized.

Despite recent agreements, the federal government and the Assembly of First Nations are involved in ongoing negotiations for the education of First Nations students. The apology by Stephen Harper on behalf of the federal government to students of residential schools (Aboriginal Affairs and Northern Development Canada, 2008c), and the strong voice among First Nations leaders for the right to collective self-determination, reflects a growing movement towards a new relationship between Aboriginal peoples and the federal government. The steady increase of alternative provisions and autonomy for schooling specifically addressing the educational aims of Aboriginal peoples and communities is indicative of this new relationship. Per-student funding levels for students attending on-reserve schools is well below the provincial and territorial average, and most First Nations leaders believe that their communities do not receive sufficient federal support for the preservation of their traditional languages, cultures, and spiritual customs. First Nations leaders are calling for substantive reforms to the current system of education for First Nations students in Canada.

Official Bilingualism in Canada

The 1960s were a time of upheaval and rapid social and political change in Quebec. This period, known as the Quiet Revolution (*Révolution tranquille*), was characterized by increasing secularism and rejection of the traditional Catholic values that had dominated Quebec up until this time. Under the banner "Masters in our own house" (*"Maître chez nous"*), political leaders sought to redefine Quebec's place in the federation, demanding greater political autonomy from the federal government. This period also saw the rise of a growing sovereignty movement in the province calling for outright independence from Anglo Canada and the British authority that resided in the British North America Act.[1] The roots of this movement were grounded in grievances the Quebecois had about their unequal treatment by the federal government. For example, in the late 1960s, French-speaking Canadians composed 25% of the population but occupied only 9% of jobs in the federal civil service (Government of Canada, 1969a, p. 374). Calls for greater autonomy or independence also stemmed from complaints that many businesses and industrial enterprises in the province were controlled by non-Quebecois who tended to hire anglophones in management positions. Tensions boiled over in 1970 when a revolutionary wing of the sovereignty movement, the Front de libération du Québec (FLQ), kidnapped British Trade Commissioner James Cross and Quebec Minister of Labour Pierre Laporte. In what would be called the October Crisis, the FLQ executed Pierre Laporte. In response, the prime minister at the time, Pierre Trudeau, enacted the War Measures Act, which gave the government the power to deploy Canadian military forces throughout the region and arrest and detain close to 500 people without bail.

In response to the rising tide of separatist sentiment in Quebec, Prime Minister Trudeau introduced a series of measures to better recognize and accommodate Quebec's demands. In 1969, Trudeau enacted the Official Languages Act (Office of the Commissioner of Official Languages,

---

1 The British North America Act, 1867, was an act of British Parliament, and changes to legislation could be made only in Britain. It was not until 1982 when Queen Elizabeth II signed the Canada Act that Canada gained control over its Constitution, which included the Charter of Rights and Freedoms.

2015), whereby French and English were given equal status in all federal institutions, including Parliament, federal bureaucracies, and Crown corporations. This law made Canada an officially bilingual country, requiring federal public institutions to provide services in both French and English. In a speech to Parliament, Trudeau described his rationale for introducing the act:

> French Canada can survive not by turning in on itself but by reaching out to claim its full share of every aspect of Canadian life. English Canada should not attempt to crush or expect to absorb French Canada. All Canadians should capitalize on the advantages of living in a country which has learned to speak in two great world languages. (Government of Canada, 1968, para 12)

In an effort to further entrench Canada's bilingual nature, Trudeau introduced the Canadian Charter of Rights and Freedoms (Government of Canada, 2014a), which included key provisions to protect the rights of the two official language groups. Section 23 of the Charter provides constitutional protection for anglophone and francophone citizens to have their children receive publically funded primary and secondary schooling in their respective official languages regardless of where they reside in Canada. Where numbers warrant, provincial and territorial governments are obliged to make provisions for French-language schools, and Quebec must provide publically funded English-language schools.

The right to have access to and provisions for publically funded French- and English-language schools, however, has limitations. In Quebec, a child has the right to access public education in English only if a parent or sibling learned English as his or her first language and it is still understood. In the rest of Canada, a child has the right to access public education in French if a parent or sibling was educated in French or if a parent has French as his or her first language and can speak fluently. Notably, these rights are not extended to non-French-speaking immigrants to Quebec, who have access only to publically funded French-language schools. However, French-speaking immigrants have the right to access publically funded French-language schools outside Quebec. In all cases, provisions for minority-language instruction are limited to areas with sufficient numbers of students to warrant such programs or facilities. Enrolment in francophone or anglophone public schools varies across Canada. For example, in relation to the percentage of students within a province attending a francophone school, only 0.4% of the student population attends in Newfoundland and Labrador, while in New

Brunswick 28.2% of the student population attends because of the large Acadian population there (Clemens et al., 2014).

Another consequence of Canada's official bilingualism policy has been the introduction and rise of French immersion schools and programs across the country. After the introduction of the Official Languages Act in 1969, many non-francophone parents became increasingly interested in having their children learn Canada's second official language (Alberta Education, 2012). Since the late 1970s, French immersion schools have been established in every provincial and territorial jurisdiction of education across the country except Quebec. Anglophone parents in Quebec wanting to have their children educated in French must enter the mainstream francophone public school system.

Currently, there are three main types of French immersion programs: early French immersion, middle French immersion, and late French immersion. Early French immersion begins in kindergarten or grade 1, while middle French immersion usually begins in grade 3, and late French immersion generally begins in grade 6 (Doyle, 2012). Instruction in these programs is provided primarily in French; however, students generally take a language arts class in English. In late immersion programs, students often take 75% of their classes in French. Generally, the extent of French-language instruction decreases as students reach high school because many courses required for university entrance, such as advanced chemistry and math, are offered only in English.

Today, French immersion programs for children who are not native French speakers are some of the most highly funded programs in public school systems across Canada. One reason for this is that French immersion programs are eligible to receive federal funding as part of initiatives to support French-language learning in Canada. However, this federal funding support is "subject to approval of Protocol of Agreements for Minority-Language Education and Second-Language Instruction" (British Columbia Ministry of Education, 2014, p. 1). French immersion programs are also one of the most popular forms of school choice offered in Canada. Statistics gathered by Canadian Parents for French indicated total enrolment in French immersion programs across Canada in 1997 at about 315,000 students, while in 2003 over 324,000 students were enrolled; the largest number of children participating was in New Brunswick (Holmes, 2008, p. 200). Numbers gathered in 2010 showed a slight decrease to 305,000 Canadian students enrolled in French immersion programs (Canadian Parents for French, 2010). These more recent numbers, which reveal that about 7% of all Canadian students are currently enrolled in a French immersion program, are impressive considering that Quebec does not offer this program.

Although French immersion programs are offered in every province and territory outside Quebec, their accessibility depends on the school district. For example, during the 2011–12 school year in Alberta, approximately 50 communities offered French immersion programs through 26 public school districts, 16 separate school districts, and 4 private schools, with total enrolment of 35,000 students (Alberta Education, 2012). One of the most impressive statistics resulting from the success of French immersion in Canada relates to the estimated 25% of people ages 18 to 29 in Canada who are considered fully bilingual, which is the highest rate of bilingualism in this age category of any country in the world (Doyle, 2012).

Notwithstanding these successes, access to French-language instruction remains a contentious issue among some francophone parents residing outside Quebec, including Acadian, Franco-Albertan, and Franco-Ontarian parents. While non-French-speaking parents often view French immersion programs as an opportunity to enrich their children's education, francophone parents tend to view French-language education as a matter of cultural and linguistic survival. Some francophone parents have become concerned that French immersion programs dedicated to families for whom French is viewed as an additional language or enrichment have taken attention away from the need to preserve the francophone identity in Canada. Consequently, these parents have advocated for more control over the governance of francophone schools. These demands were highlighted in the case of Mahe v. Alberta (1990). Under Section 23 of the Charter, Mahe challenged the provincial government for failing to create a francophone school board. The Supreme Court ruled in the family's favour, determining that where numbers warranted, "entitlement to minority language education could extend beyond the provision of the physical facility of the school, to include a degree of management and control by minority language citizens over the minority school system" (Supreme Court of Canada, 2008, para. 28).

This landmark case provided for the establishment of separate francophone public school boards in Alberta. Consequently, along with the presence of public francophone school boards in every province and territory, the current Canadian educational landscape includes separate francophone school boards in Alberta and Ontario. However, Alberta has only one separate francophone school board (in Calgary), with 951 students in the system (Clemens et al., 2014, p. 18). Ontario, in contrast,

Table 1. Distribution of Anglophone, Francophone, and French Immersion Schools

Province or territory	Anglophone public	Francophone public	Separate francophone	French immersion
British Columbia	✔	✔		✔
Alberta	✔	✔	✔	✔
Saskatchewan	✔	✔		✔
Manitoba	✔	✔		✔
Ontario	✔	✔	✔	✔
Quebec	✔	✔		
New Brunswick	✔	✔		✔
Nova Scotia	✔	✔		✔
Prince Edward Island	✔	✔		✔
Newfoundland & Labrador	✔	✔		✔
Yukon, Northwest Territories, Nunavut	✔	✔		✔

has eight separate francophone school boards across the province, educating 70,278 students (Clemens et al., 2014, p. 18). Table 1 outlines the French immersion program possibilities across Canada, along with the provinces and territories that offer francophone and anglophone parents the choice of attending separate official language schools.

These constitutional developments clearly demonstrate that preserving the French language has been an integral part of the Canadian educational reality since Trudeau introduced policies that made Canada a bilingual country. Although the French language and francophone culture have become a core part of the Canadian identity, citizens do not have to speak both official languages, nor does federal legislation ensure the protection of either official language at the provincial level. New Brunswick is the only officially bilingual province in Canada, and Quebec is officially unilingual (French only). More recently, the languages of the other national minority group in Canada, Aboriginal peoples, have been gaining increased recognition, particularly at the territorial level. In addition to English, Inuktitut is also the official language of Nunavut, and nine Aboriginal languages have official status in the Northwest Territories.

Conclusion

Although many school choice reforms in the Western world emerged during the 1980s and 1990s in response to the neoliberal discourse of the Reagan and Thatcher administrations, Canadian school choice policies are embedded in the foundations of Confederation and realized in the Constitution Act, 1867. The right to publically funded separate schools for French Roman Catholics and English Protestants was negotiated in 1867 and forms the basis for the Catholic and public school boards that currently operate in various provinces. These early measures, along with more recent language rights guaranteed in the Charter of Rights and Freedoms, have greatly influenced the direction the school choice movement has taken across the country. School choice policies in Canada have included debates regarding autonomy and control of education for Aboriginal communities; however, the problem of clearly defining Aboriginal educational rights remains unresolved, as evidenced by per-student funding for Aboriginal students attending on-reserve schools that is well below provincial and territorial averages. In summary, both early and later constitutional provisions in Canada have provided national minority groups with various accommodations and degrees of control over how their children are educated.

Some of the major historical and political milestones that have influenced and shaped school choice policies in relation to national minority groups in Canada include the following:

1 The Constitution Act of 1867 adopted federalism as a means to devolve powers to the provincial level so that the French-speaking Quebecois could have control over education within their historic territory.
2 The Constitution Act introduced legal provisions to protect the minority religious rights of Protestants in Quebec and Roman Catholics in Ontario and later Alberta, Saskatchewan, and Newfoundland.
3 The Constitution Act provided no rights or protections for the diverse languages, cultures, and traditions of Aboriginal peoples of Canada. Through various provisions in the Indian Act, including the introduction of residential schools, the federal government sought to assimilate Aboriginal peoples into the dominant Anglo-Canadian culture. Since the early 1970s, Aboriginal peoples have gained increasing control and influence over education to ensure that the

schools their children attend offer more culturally and linguistically appropriate teaching and learning environments.

4 Flowing from provisions in the Official Languages Act of 1969, and later entrenched in Section 23 of the Canadian Charter of Rights and Freedoms, anglophone and francophone citizens were afforded the right to have their children receive publically funded primary and secondary schooling in their respective official languages regardless of where in Canada they reside.

5 The introduction of the Official Languages Act led to the rise of French immersion schools and programs across the country, making it one of the most popular alternative education programs in Canada.

3

Educational Accommodations
for Other Minority Groups

In Chapter 2, we explored constitutional and legal provisions that have been negotiated by Canada's national minority communities, the Quebecois and Aboriginal peoples, to preserve their unique cultural and linguistic identities. In this chapter we examine parallel calls by immigrant minority groups for greater recognition and accommodation of their distinct identities. As noted previously, immigrant minority groups differ from national minority groups in that they "are the result not of involuntary incorporation of complete societies settled in their historical lands, but of the decisions of individuals and families to leave their original homeland for a new life" (Kymlicka, 1998, p. 7). In choosing to immigrate to Canada, immigrant groups understand they are entering a new country with already established laws and institutions. As a result, immigrant groups have not historically called for, nor attained, forms of self-government or collective autonomy. Rather, they have demanded, and to varying degrees secured, fairer terms for integration into the dominant society through accommodations for their ethnocultural identities.

This chapter comprises three sections. In the first section, we outline ways in which immigrant groups were historically subjected to various assimilatory policies within education. We examine how the introduction of the Canadian Charter of Rights and Freedoms in 1982, as well as the Canadian Multiculturalism Act in 1988, provided new regulatory frameworks for integrating new arrivals into Canadian society. We discuss the tensions inherent in finding a balance between recognizing and accommodating cultural differences within a society while also ensuring unity and social cohesion.

In the second section, we explore how educational jurisdictions have responded to the demands by religious minority groups for specific cultural accommodations under the legislation referred to above. We outline how provisions in the Charter have forced public schools to abandon formerly common Christian practices and religious schools to alter their educational practices so as not to discriminate against minority groups such as the lesbian, gay, bisexual, and transgendered (LGBT) community. Next, we discuss the extent to which religious minority groups have been able to secure public funding to establish faith-based and heritage-language schools. We end this section by outlining how provincial and territorial educational jurisdictions have become more responsive to recognizing and incorporating minority cultural traditions and identities.

In the final section, we outline how Quebec has largely rejected the principles of multiculturalism. In its place, Quebec has offered interculturalism as a viable framework for balancing the requirements of integration against the imperatives of respecting diversity. We conclude the chapter by discussing how, in light of the philosophical principles of interculturalism, Quebec has responded to demands for reasonable accommodation in educational spaces.

Accommodating Diversity through Multiculturalism

Beginning in the late nineteenth century, the federal government undertook a series of measures to increase Canada's population. From 1896 to 1914, the Canadian government encouraged European immigration to populate and farm western Canada. Of the three million people who immigrated to Canada during this time, more than 800,000 were of neither French nor British origin (Richardson, 2002). In response to the growing ethnic diversity of the country, largely because of immigration from Eastern and Northern Europe, provincial educational jurisdictions in Canada sought to assimilate minority immigrant cultural traditions into the values of the Anglo-Saxon Protestant elite that dominated Canada outside Quebec. The primary aim of public schools in English-speaking Canada was to create a homogenous nation built on a common English language and shared cultural values realized through promoting identification with British institutions and practices. A school superintendent in Canada West speaking in 1896, for example, warned: "If these [immigrants'] children are to grow up as Canadian citizens they must be led to adopt our viewpoint and speak our speech ... A common school and common tongue are necessary if we are to have a homogenous citizenship" (as quoted in Titley & Miller, 1982, p. 132). Because of these strongly assimilatory educational policies, early immigrants to Canada were expected to quickly assimilate into the mainstream culture and were encouraged to let go of their traditional cultures and languages.

This situation began to change during the turmoil and increased intellectual dissent of the 1960s. Through grassroots social movements, immigrant minority groups increasingly contested the orthodoxies and received values of the Anglo establishment. Based on the principles of human rights and social justice, these groups called for increased rights and freedoms for religious, cultural, and linguistic expression. Seeking to respond to these demands in a way that would recognize the increasing ethnic diversity of the country, in 1971, Prime Minister Trudeau introduced a new policy, "Bilingualism within a Multicultural Framework," as the basis for a new organizing ideal for Canadian citizenship. In a speech to the House of Commons at this time, Trudeau articulated the rationale for this new federal policy:

> There cannot be one cultural policy for Canadians of British and French origin, another for the original peoples and yet another for all others. For although there are two official languages, there is no official culture, nor does any ethnic group take precedence over any other ... We are free to be ourselves ... It is the policy of this government ... to "safeguard" this freedom ... A policy of multiculturalism within a bilingual framework commends itself to the government as the most suitable means of assuring the cultural freedom of Canadians. (Canada History, 2013, p. 1)

Through this legislative framework, Canada became the first country in the world to have an official policy of multiculturalism at the federal level (Kymlicka, 1998).

Following the introduction of this federal statute, Trudeau went on to enact the Canadian Charter of Rights and Freedoms in 1982, which enshrined these sentiments into the Canadian constitutional framework. These views can be seen, for example, in Section 27, which states that "this Charter shall be interpreted in a manner consistent with the preservation and enhancement of the multicultural heritage of Canadians" (Government of Canada, 2014a). Beyond recognizing French and English as the two official languages of Canada, as well as the rights of Aboriginal communities gained through previous treaty agreements, the Charter guarantees equality rights for all citizens, including the right to the equal protection and equal benefit of the law "without discrimination based on race, national or ethnic origin, colour, religion, sex, age or mental or physical disability" (Government of Canada, 2014a, Section 15.1).

The principles of multiculturalism were further affirmed in 1988 with the introduction of the Canadian Multiculturalism Act. With this piece of legislation, the official policy of the Government of Canada acknowledges "the freedom of all members of Canadian society to preserve, enhance and share their cultural heritage" (Government of Canada, 2014b, Section 3.1[a]). By affirming multiculturalism as a fundamental characteristic of Canadian heritage and identity, this act seeks to ensure that individuals and communities of all origins are able to participate fully in Canadian society. The act states that barriers inhibiting their ability to do so should be eliminated. The act also asserts the government's policy to encourage Canadian institutions, including schools, to be "both respectful and inclusive of Canada's multicultural character" (Government of Canada, 2014b, Section 3.1[f]). While the act affirms the status of Canada's official languages, it also addresses federal policy to "preserve and enhance the use of languages other than English and French" (Government of Canada, 2014b, Section 3.1[i]).

Early advocates of this constitutional and policy framework "saw it as the best way to protect both individuals and minorities by imposing firm limits on 'the tyranny of the majority' and the state's ability to interfere with personal freedom" (Centre for Research and Information on Canada, 2002, p. 4). Advocates of this policy framework have additionally highlighted the necessity of recognizing the identities of people who have not historically been part of the dominant group. C. Taylor (1994) wrote:

> The demand for recognition in [the politics of multiculturalism] is given urgency by the supposed links between recognition and identity ... The thesis is that our identity is partly shaped by recognition or its absence, often by misrecognition of others, and so a person or group of people can suffer real damage, real distortion, if the people or society around them mirror back to them a confining or demeaning or contemptible picture of themselves. Non-recognition or misrecognition can be a form of oppression, imprisoning someone in a false, distorted or reduced mode of being. (p. 25)

An educative directive is implicit in this statement. If the state remains passive in the role of facilitating the recognition of a person's identity, the potential for misrecognition or an absence of recognition may have an adverse effect on that person. This position has three normative implications. First, individuals ought to be able to foster their cultural identities within the public sphere as civic equals. Second, an individual might require certain educational accommodations to facilitate this recognition of his or her identity. Third, the recognition of identity may need to be done in a substantive and meaningful way involving specialized educational programs. These implications create the impetus for the state to fund heritage-language programs and alternative programs and schools that recognize and promote particular cultural and religious identities.

Although the principles of multiculturalism support the creation of such schools, liberal democracies also have a responsibility and desire to sustain a collective identity among all citizens so as to foster group cohesion and feelings of attachment to the country. These attributes lend legitimacy to the state's institutions and compel its citizens to pay taxes, obey the laws, and participate in the democratic life of their community. Public schools are one of the primary spaces where a common set of values and beliefs are forged. Accordingly, public schools are intended to bring children together from varied backgrounds to interact and learn from one another in a respectful environment. Advocates of the common school approach argue that these interactions heighten tolerance and understanding among different groups because more advantaged children in particular will see "others" (stigmatized, "minoritized" peoples) as moral equals and fellow citizens with roughly equal rights and opportunities (Merry, 2012).

Thus, liberal democracies such as Canada that value pluralism are presented with the dual challenge of recognizing and affirming the multiple identities of all citizens while also creating and transmitting a common set of beliefs, values, and sense of collective identity (Bouchard, 2001; McAndrew, 2001). One of the central places where this tension finds meaning and expression is within public schools. The introduction of the Charter of Rights and Freedoms and the Canadian Multiculturalism Act raised important educational policy considerations regarding the kinds of reasonable accommodations that would be made for immigrant minority cultures, languages, and religions. For example, "How far should the right to freedom of religion, freedom of thought, freedom of belief, and freedom of expression intrude into public space when they compromise fundamental human rights such as equality?" (Stein, 2007, p. 12). Is it reasonable for independent Islamic schools that teach the provincially or territorially mandated curriculum to be eligible for government funding if they segregate girls in separate classrooms for religious reasons? Because education is strictly under the authority of provincial and territorial governments in Canada, considerable variation has occurred in how they have responded to these types of questions. The Charter of Rights and Freedoms and the Canadian Multiculturalism Act provide the legal and philosophical foundation from which ministries of education and school boards react to demands and situations that highlight the tension between recognizing and preserving a shared set of values while also ensuring the individual rights of all citizens to maintain and preserve their unique cultural identities.

The Impact of the Charter and the Multiculturalism Act on Schools

Religious rights in schools, particularly among non-Christian groups, have received a significant amount of public attention. The global resurgence of religious orthodoxy has challenged governments to create legislation that determines limits of reasonable accommodation for the religious rights of minority groups. The task has been particularly difficult in relation to communities whose religions are integral to their culture and identity, but whose religious values challenge both the ethos of the dominant culture and, in some cases, the fundamental liberal democratic principles that inform Canadian policies.

One case that highlights this challenge occurred in Quebec, where the court system was asked to rule on whether an orthodox Sikh boy should be permitted to wear his ceremonial Sikh dagger – the *kirpan* – in school, even though the publically funded school he was attending strictly forbade students from carrying weapons of any kind. While the Quebec court ruled in favour of the school's decision not allowing him to do so, the case went to the Supreme Court (Gereluk & Scott, 2014). In a unanimous decision, the Supreme Court ruled that the boy should be able to wear his ceremonial dagger but with strict guidelines (i.e., the kirpan had to be wrapped and sewn in a sturdy cloth envelope and worn under clothing; Gereluk, 2008).

This case brought to light the principles of reasonable accommodation that minority cultural practices are afforded within the Charter of Rights and Freedoms. Specifically, the court asserted that the state has a duty to adjust, accommodate, and make alternative arrangements with particular individuals or groups to reduce discriminatory practices. The rationale is that identical treatment for all people often does not reduce the level of discrimination commonly felt by minority groups. Based on these principles, the Supreme Court stated that "unless the school could show that the kirpan would cause undue hardship to others, then reasonable accommodation should be applied to protect the boy's religious freedom" (Gereluk, 2008, p. 66). In safeguarding and maintaining Canadian multicultural values, the Supreme Court felt that providing a "total prohibition" (as quoted in Gereluk, 2008, p. 66) of the kirpan would send the wrong message, suggesting that some religious symbols held more weight and privilege than others.

Other groups in Canada have called for accommodations in schools to support their unique identities. The need for schools to respond to these accommodations has been highlighted by Zine's (2000) research on Islamic subcultures in Ontario schools. In her study, Zine found that members of stigmatized minority groups, such as Muslim students, experience the secular, Eurocentric focus of Canadian education as alienating because their cultural and religious practices run counter to the conventional standards of the dominant culture (2000, p. 293). She found that some students develop a split personality syndrome or double identity "in order to contend with the reality of integration within the dominant society, and at the same time attempt to maintain the integrity of their identity and lifestyle as Muslims" (Zine, 2000, p. 293). The same could be said of other faith groups, such as Christians, Jews, or Hindus, whose religious practice is paramount to their identity, or LGBT students.[1] As a result, these groups have called for institutional conditions to support voluntary subcultures in schools that foster the development of supportive "social networks that nourish and sustain [them] and provide a sense of belonging and attachment essential for personal happiness and well-being" (Merry, 2012, p. 89).

Ontario provides an interesting case study to examine the degree to which institutional accommodations should be introduced in schools, even when certain religious practices compromise fundamental human rights such as equality. In neighbourhoods where children of marginalized minority groups constitute the majority in public schools, educators in Ontario were tasked with accommodating the cultural values and traditions of that community. For example, at Valley Park Middle School in Toronto, over 90% of the student population is Muslim. In 2008 the school administration introduced a prayer program in the cafeteria after lunchtime because students were leaving to attend mosque and were not coming back to school. On Fridays, local imams are brought in to lead

---

1 In 1996 the Toronto School Board established the Triangle Program to provide a "class-room where Lesbian, Gay, Bisexual and Transgender (LGBT) youth can learn and earn credits in a safe, harassment-free, equity-based environment, and developing and teaching curriculum which includes and celebrates LGBT literature, history, persons and issues" (Triangle Program's mission statement, as cited in Ekwa-Ekoko, 2008, p. 27).

a traditional 40-minute service for about 400 students during which the boys sit in front of the girls. Non-Muslims are banned from the room during prayers.

However, such accommodations were not without protest from other religious and community groups. In July 2011, the Canadian Hindu Advocacy, Christian Heritage Party, and Jewish Defence League joined in protest to call for a stop to Muslim prayers in public schools (Davidson, 2011; Godfrey, 2011a, 2011b; Yuen, 2011a, 2011b). They argued that permitting Muslim prayers during school hours in a publically funded school was a violation of fundamental Canadian values and that religious accommodation should not be made for one group and not others. They questioned why public schools could no longer celebrate religious traditions of the dominant Christian majority, such as Easter or Christmas, yet could provide space for Muslim prayer. Other groups reasoned that traditional Muslim prayer violated gender equality – a fundamental value in Canadian society – by requiring girls to sit behind boys and relegating menstruating girls to the very back of the room. Alia Hogben, executive director of the Canadian Council of Muslim Women, argued that public schools should be teaching kids how to be Canadian and called for more supervision and guidance of prayer sessions in schools. Hogben echoed the sentiment of concerned parents in questioning who was assessing what the imams were teaching these children when only Muslim parents were supervising these sessions (Davidson, 2011, para. 12). Meir Weinstein of the Jewish Defence League voiced his concern that radical or fundamental imams could be indoctrinating these students with views not conducive to social harmony or citizenship in a liberal democracy and in conflict with Canadian values (Godfrey, 2011a). The Toronto District School Board is clear on its role in making these accommodations. The board provides the space for prayers, but the administration is not involved with the prayers itself; rather, this is the responsibility of the parents of that community.

Seeking a more uniform policy in response to this debate, the Ontario Ministry of Education approved a report, *Developing and Implementing Equity and Inclusive Education Policies in Ontario Schools* (Ontario Ministry of Education, 2011), requiring all public and Catholic school boards to develop policies to "foster respecting diversity, promoting inclusive education, and identifying and eliminating discriminatory biases, systemic barriers, and power dynamics that limit students' learning, growth, and contribution to society" (p. 19). This document paid specific attention to such factors "as race, sexual orientation, physical or mental disability, gender, and class that can intersect to create additional barriers for some students" (Ontario Ministry of Education, 2011, p. 119). The most contentious area of this policy document responded to the debates about religious accommodation that sanctioned a number of schools in the Toronto District School Board providing time and space for Muslim prayers on Friday afternoon. The Ontario Human Rights Commissioner was clear that both public and Catholic school boards must accommodate the needs of faith groups, including permitting religious services, provided these do not interfere with the primary goal of educating students.

Secularization of schools

While these case studies highlight the kinds of religious accommodations deemed reasonable considering the rights guaranteed in the Charter of Rights and Freedoms, since the introduction of the Charter there has been marked movement away from allowing religious cultural practices in schools reflective of the formerly dominant Christian community. Before the Charter, for example, it was common for schools across Canada to allow daily school prayers. However, this situation changed in public schools in Ontario with the precedent of Zylberberg v. Sudbury Board of Education (1988). This case centred on whether having students recite the Lord's Prayer and receive Bible lessons infringed on non-Christians' religious freedoms. The Ontario Court of Appeal ruled that having students recite the Lord's Prayer in a public school did infringe on non-Christians' freedom of religious rights, and therefore parents who did not approve of this practice could exempt their children from this daily routine.

The school justified these daily rituals as a way to develop children's sense of citizenship and moral values. However, the non-Christian defendants argued that those who asked for exemption from participating in the daily prayers would be discriminated against and would therefore feel pressured to observe the daily ritual for fear of being stigmatized. The appeals court ruled that the school did not need to rely on the Lord's Prayer to foster a sense of citizenship and moral values; instead, the court felt that the school could provide alternative activities to develop educational and moral values, which would not infringe on the rights of non-Christians. The reversal of provisions for daily prayer was taken up by most provincial jurisdictions thereafter, requiring amendments to their school acts that previously accommodated Christian practices to the exclusion of other faiths and beliefs. This early decision to remove the daily prayer in public schools protected non-Christians within the dominant moral norms taught in schools. The case of Zylberberg v. Sudbury Board of Education (1988) ultimately contributed to making public schools across Canada more secular by removing schools' ability to maintain Christian rituals and traditions.

Calls for Catholic schools to accommodate groups and identity positions historically not in line with Catholic values, emanating from content in both the Charter and the Canadian Multiculturalism Act, have also succeeded. In June 2012, the Government of Ontario passed Bill 13, the Accepting Schools Act, which additionally affected the autonomy of publically funded Catholic schools. This bill established anti-bullying legislation premised on the belief that

> all students should feel safe at school and deserve a positive school climate that is inclusive and accepting, regardless of race, ancestry, place of origin, colour, ethnic origin, citizenship, creed, sex, sexual orientation, gender identity, gender expression, age, marital status, family status or disability. (Government of Ontario, 2012, ch. 5, para. 3)

While many lauded the spirit of the legislation in terms of fostering tolerance, this policy remains contentious for publically funded Catholic schools that are obliged to permit the establishment of gay–straight alliance clubs on student request, even when these clubs are not endorsed by the community or parents.

This legislation highlights the extent to which school choice mandates must be balanced within the larger democratic and liberal values that society requires all its citizens to uphold. Under the matrix of reasonable accommodation, even if students choose to attend a Catholic school, the school still has an obligation to protect the well-being of all students. Both the anti-bullying and gay–straight alliance directives are overt measures by the state to ensure protection of students' sexual orientation in public spaces. In Ontario, parents and students cannot simply opt out by choosing a school that limits such discussions. A balance must be maintained between the discretion of families to choose schools with a particular value system and the greater democratic role of the state to protect individual rights for the common good of citizens in society.

In Alberta, the government has granted parents greater control and autonomy regarding whether they want their children to be exposed to certain controversial or sensitive issues in school. Section 11.1 of the Alberta Human Rights Act (commonly referred to in the media as Bill

44) requires schools to provide prior written notice to parents when subject matter related to religion, human sexuality, or sexual orientation is primarily and explicitly addressed in the curriculum (Gereluk, 2011). Parents may exempt their child from such discussions. This accommodation is reflective of the sociopolitical context of Alberta schools and consistent with the government's position of transferring responsibility to parents to make choices regarding their children's socialization.

The case of faith-based schools

The growing secularization of schools around a shared set of liberal democratic values reflects the view that public schools should be largely passive regarding accommodations for cultural identity and instead should strive to unify children, regardless of their cultural or religious affiliations. However, some schools have worked to accommodate minority religions, particularly when that religion is a demographic majority within a school. With an increase in the number of immigrants to Canada from displaced communities for whom religious affiliation defines their culture and identity, some minority groups have called for state funding for faith-based schools. While historically publically funded faith-based schools in Canada were either Roman Catholic or Protestant, the recent request for religious schools has largely come from Islamic, Jewish, and evangelical Christian communities. Thus, another element of school choice debate in Canada concerns whether schools serving religious denominations that have not historically received constitutional protections should receive provincial and territorial funding.

People who believe that these religious schools should receive provincial funding have tried to use to the Charter of Rights and Freedoms as the basis of their argument. For example, Adler v. Ontario (1996) claimed that the decision by the Ministry of Education in Ontario not to publically fund Jewish and Christian day schools, nor include them as part of the public education system, was in violation of the Charter's guarantees of freedom of conscience and religion, as well as Charter provisions concerning the right to equality without discrimination based on religion. However, the court ruled that the historical compromises made in Section 93 of the Constitution Act to Roman Catholics and Protestants could not be expanded to include other groups under Section 2 of the Charter. "The Court of Appeal found that s. 2(*a*) of the *Charter* did not provide a positive entitlement to state support for the exercise of one's religious practice and that any infringement was justified under s. 1" (Adler v. Ontario, 1996, para. 1). As a result, Ontario did not expand religious freedoms to include public funding of religious private schools. The right for parents to demand publically funded religious schools has been complicated by the fact that some provinces and territories support publically funded Catholic school districts, creating "considerable ambiguity concerning religious rights in education" (Miller, 1986, p. 283).

Given this ruling, as well as the ambiguity regarding public funding of faith-based schools, some school districts have authorized alternative religious schools within the public education system. Manitoba, Saskatchewan, Alberta, and British Columbia have taken a more active role in the recognition of religious identity in provisions for public schooling. In addition to publically funded Catholic schools, these provinces also have partial or full funding for religious schools licensed or accredited by the government.

Since 1988, the Alberta School Act has permitted the formation of alternative programs with a religious emphasis. The Calgary Board of Education, however, does not permit the creation of alternative schools with a religious focus. In contrast, the neighbouring Palliser Regional School Division has actively accommodated faith-based alternative schools, with campuses for Christians, Mennonites, and Hutterites (Palliser Regional Schools, 2015, para. 3). Also within the Calgary region, the Almadina Language Charter Academy, established in 1996 as a second-language school, caters primarily to Islamic faith families, who constitute 95% of the school population. Along with offering daily Arabic instruction, the school accommodates Islamic rituals, customs, and traditions in its culture, organization, and management practices. The Edmonton Public School Board has provided accommodations for the Logos Society by offering five Christian alternative programs (Edmonton Logos Society, 2015). In addition, two independent Jewish schools were invited to become part of the public school board (Talmud Torah Society, 2011).These religiously affiliated schools in Edmonton and Calgary are required to follow Alberta Education curriculum in their secular subject programming.

Ontario and the Atlantic provinces do not provide any public funding for non-Catholic religious schools (see Table 2). Parents wanting to send their children to a faith-based school in these provinces can do so only by homeschooling or paying full tuition at an independent or a private school. Consequently, most religious denominations in Canada are having their schooling options met by independent schools that exist outside of public education.

Table 2. Provincial and Territorial Funding Levels for Faith-Based Schools across Canada

Province or territory	Level of funding
British Columbia	From 35% to 50% funding for schools that meet rigorous standards and teach the BC curriculum. Schools include the Vancouver Hebrew Academy, Dasmesh Punjabi School in Abbotsford, and the IQRA Islamic School in Surrey.
Alberta	Up to 60% funding for independent schools that teach the Alberta curriculum. Full funding to faith-based alternative public schools, excluding charter schools, which cannot be religiously based.
Saskatchewan	Full funding for "historical high schools," named because they were established in the early twentieth century at a time when public high schools were not available in some parts of the province. These include Luther College High School, the Mennonite School, and the Athol Murray College of Notre Dame. Full to partial funding for religious schools associated with some school districts. Funding of 3.5% for independent schools that meet rigorous provincial standards. These include the Islamic Academy of Saskatchewan and the Mother Teresa School. There are 28 unfunded faith-based schools.
Manitoba	Independent schools are eligible for 50% of funding provided to public schools for operating costs if the school complies with provincial standards. Approximately 13,000 students are enrolled in independent schools, 84% of whom are enrolled in religious schools that are predominantly Catholic. There are 45 unfunded schools, 96% of which are faith based.
Ontario	Full funding for the Catholic board only.
Quebec	In 1998, religious school boards were replaced with French and English language boards. All faith-based schools are private and eligible for 60% of the funding public schools receive if they comply with government regulations (i.e., curriculum, school inspection, student testing).
New Brunswick	No provincial funding support.
Nova Scotia	No provincial funding support.
Prince Edward Island	No provincial funding support.
Newfoundland & Labrador	No provincial funding support.
Yukon, Northwest Territories, Nunavut	No territorial funding support.

Source: Adapted from "Faith-Based Schools" by J. Wilson, 2007, *CBCNews*. Copyright 2007 by CBCNews.

Heritage-language programs

Earlier we noted that the Canadian Multiculturalism Act encourages pub-lic institutions to "preserve and enhance the use of languages other than English and French" (Government of Canada, 2014b, Section 3.1[i]). Because language immersion programs offer more robust approaches to accommodate cultural identity, some parents have called for the intro-duction of publically funded heritage-language schools, such as Ukraini-an, Mandarin, and Spanish. However, because the Canadian Multicultur-alism Act is not a constitutional document, school boards are not bound by it. In a situation similar to that of non-Catholic or non-Protestant faith-based schools, neither the Constitution Act of 1867 nor the Charter made provisions for the protection and promotion of languages other than English and French. Critics of publically funded language immer-sion programs agree with this stance, arguing that these programs are a mechanism to perpetuate cultural identity and values particular to ethnic minority groups, thereby weakening the integration of children into Canadian society. For example, the majority of students enrolled in Hebrew, Mandarin, and Punjabi language programs are from families of those ethnic groups, contributing to the creation of an exclusive homo-geneous setting.

Proponents of language immersion programs argue not only for their academic benefits but also for the important function they serve in fostering tolerance and understanding in society through exposure to social and cultural traditions of particular language groups. They also argue that learning a heritage language can strengthen the cultural her-itage of a community and sustain intergenerational dialogue between immigrants to Canada and their first- and second-generation Canadian-born children. Aside from seeking opportunities to conserve their heri-tage language, parents often choose language immersion programs as a cost-effective way to challenge their children academically and increase their opportunities for social and career advancement.

Based on such arguments, and despite the resources required to sup-port heritage-language programs, large urban school districts in the west-ern provinces have been leaders in funding heritage-language schools. A cursory review of Alberta provides an example. Following the 1969 fed-eral report of the Royal Commission on Bilingualism and Biculturalism (Government of Canada, 1969a, 1969b), in 1971 the Alberta government enacted a provision to include the instruction of languages, currently under Section 11.1 of the Alberta School Act: "A board may authorize the use of French or any other language as a language of instruction" (School Act, RSA 2000, c S-3). As a result of this legislation, Alberta hosts over 50 heritage-language schools that teach over 32 languages, with Punjabi the latest to be added. In addition to heritage-language and French immersion programs, second-language immersion programs such as Spanish and Mandarin are gaining popularity in Alberta. The Edmonton Public School Board, serving a city rich in cultural diversity, was a pioneer in creating provisions for these programs and is currently host to the majority of heritage-language programs in Alberta. As Table 3 shows, only British Columbia, Alberta, Saskatchewan, and Manitoba have laws allowing for fully funded public transitional and dual-language school programs.

Changes to classroom multicultural education

In terms of cultural accommodation for minority groups in schools, recognition can be either minimal or robust. Minimal recognition entails a passive stance; the teacher takes into consideration a child's cultural background or identity without necessarily calling attention to any special features but is sensitive to how this identity might affect the child's response to certain situations (Feinberg, 1998, p. 169). For example, this recognition might be reflected in appropriate classroom management practices, selection of curricular resources, accommodation for voluntary nonparticipation in certain activities because of religious conventions, or permission to wear religious symbols.

Feinberg (1998) argued that robust recognition requires teachers to

> take active steps to engage the child in a way that will strengthen her affiliation to a given cultural group ... It requires the teacher to steer the child toward a certain kind of membership and help her develop an *identity as a person of this kind.* (pp. 169–170, emphasis added)

For example, the Toronto District School Board established Africentric alternative schools with the aim to integrate "the histories, cultures, experiences and contributions of people of African descent and other racialized groups into the curriculum, teaching methodologies, and social environment of schools" (Toronto District School Board, 2008, as quoted in Chen, 2010, p. 2) and the Triangle Program as a safe, inclusive setting for LGBT students. Robust recognition also requires teachers to teach "children outside the targeted group to understand

Table 3. Provincial and Territorial Heritage-Language Program Funding

Province or territory	Heritage-language program funding
British Columbia	Full publically funded bilingual programs within certain school districts in English–Mandarin and English–Russian.
Alberta	Full publically funded bilingual programs within certain school districts in English–Arabic, English–American Sign Language, English–Mandarin, English–German, English–Hebrew, English–Spanish, and English–Ukrainian.
Saskatchewan	Full publically funded bilingual programs within certain school districts in English–Ukrainian.
Manitoba	Full publically funded bilingual programs within certain school districts in English–Ukrainian, English–Hebrew, and English–German.
Ontario	No provincial funding support.
Quebec	No provincial funding support.
New Brunswick	No provincial funding support.
Nova Scotia	No provincial funding support.
Prince Edward Island	No provincial funding support.
Newfoundland & Labrador	No provincial funding support.
Yukon, Northwest Territories, Nunavut	No territorial funding support.

and appreciate cultural practices that are specific to the culture of the marginalized student" (Feinberg, 1998, p. 170), to foster tolerance and intergroup harmony.

While many attempts to address multiculturalism and cultural identity in public schools are sincere and well intentioned, advocates of multicultural approaches to education want authentic forms of recognition that transcend cultural heritage celebrations of food, dance, and festivals. At the classroom level, recognizing and honouring cultural diversity can involve opening up curricula to encompass a wider range of materials from the perspectives of people who have been historically silenced in schools to foster attitudinal changes in both students and teachers. This recognition includes incorporating materials from Aboriginal perspectives and the perspective of other marginalized groups, such as women, the special needs community, and Canadians of Asian and African descent. Recognizing diversity in the classroom "aims at fostering pride in minority cultures, helping students from minority groups develop new insights into their respective cultures, reducing stereotyping and prejudice, and promoting intercultural understanding" (Egea-Kuehne, 2012, p. 138).

A tension exists between robust and minimal recognition in terms of cultural accommodation in Canada. Some policymakers suggest that people who have chosen to leave a country to seek a new life elsewhere have, in effect, implicitly waived their rights to have their group identity maintained through public resources; however, they recognize that children of voluntary immigrants have the right to minimum recognition (Feinberg, 1998, p. 171). The same would be true regarding accommodation for gender orientation and special needs students.

The case of Quebec

Quebec is unique regarding accommodations for culture and identity in public schools. The Supreme Court decision allowing the orthodox Sikh boy to wear his ceremonial dagger at a Quebec school (notably with strict guidelines) led to a media storm of opposition in the province (Gereluk, 2008). Many people in Quebec believed this ruling went too far in accommodating minority groups. Specifically, these kinds of accommodations left the door open for dangerous and illiberal practices that threaten the established liberal democratic nature of Quebec society. Policymakers in Quebec responded with the conceptual framework of interculturalism, which lays out the limits of how much a host society should be willing to accommodate cultural and religious differences. The Bouchard-Taylor report (Bouchard & Taylor, 2008) defined interculturalism as follows:

> We could say that Quebec Interculturalism a) institutes French as the common language of intercultural relations; b) cultivates a pluralist orientation that is highly sensitive to the protections of rights; c) preserves the creative tension between diversity and the continuity of the French-speaking core and the social link; d) places special emphasis on integration; and e) advocates interaction. (p. 17)

In advancing these principles, the Government of Quebec asks new arrivals to enter into a moral contract with their host community "to further the basic societal values of individual rights and freedoms, democratic participation, the promotion of a common public language, openness to plurality, and intercultural dialogue" (Maxwell, Waddington,

McDonough, Cormier, & Schwimmer, 2012, p. 34). In shifting the focus away from an exclusive emphasis on the responsibility of established citizens to welcome and accept newcomers, interculturalism also places an emphasis on the newcomers' responsibility to adapt and integrate into the dominant social, linguistic, and cultural reality of the society they are entering. Notably, this approach is asymmetrical in the sense that values and practices of newly arrived immigrant peoples do not carry the same weight as the already established community. The "ideal is of a balanced but asymmetrical give-and-take of adjustment, exchanges, and compromise between the home society and those of new arrivals" (Maxwell et al., 2012, p. 434).

The emphasis is on sharing dialogue to create a larger collective civic project. By taking part in a shared dialogue, proponents of interculturalism see the ways diverse peoples and perspectives can work to enrich and jointly build a common culture. In the case of Quebec, the francophone community may be vulnerable to threats by the surrounding Canadian and American anglophone culture. A resistance by heterogeneous minority groups to integrate with the majority French culture's values, learn the French language, and adhere to French civil law further exacerbates this vulnerability. Although plurality and diversity among minority groups are recognized in Quebec, a tension exists between the majority culture's continued ability to maintain stability and the claims by diverse groups' for their own sense of identity. In the politics of recognition and concern for integration, the majority culture is vigilant in preserving its legitimacy within a common public culture. Thus, public schools in Quebec focus primarily on civic responsibilities and the preservation of the majority French culture and are largely passive with regard to accommodations for other cultural identities. Public schools strive to unify children regardless of their cultural affiliations. Families and individuals are left to pursue their own cultural meaning and traditions in their homes, communities, and places of worship, and they have the option of sending their children to private schools. The aim is to create a coexistence among majority and minority cultures with a particular pluralist view of maintaining the values underpinned by the "host society" (Maxwell et al., 2012, p. 429).

Despite the restrictive laws related to religion and language education, Quebec has the highest proportion of students enrolled in private schools in Canada, with students in English-language schools accounting for 12% of total enrolment in private schools (Allison & Van Pelt, 2012). The government maintains tight regulations regarding the operation of private schools, ensuring they teach the provincially mandated curriculum. Private Jewish, Muslim, and Christian schools are required to teach an ethics and religious culture course that provides nonpreferential descriptive accounts of religion. The provincial government takes decisive action when schools are not adhering to provincial curriculum standards. In 2006, after an inquiry into allegations that an evangelical independent school was not following the provincial curriculum, the Minister of Education mandated that all schools in the province, including independent, religiously affiliated, licensed, or unlicensed schools, must follow the content of the prescribed provincial curriculum, including instruction in sex education and Darwin's theory of evolution (Stein, 2007, p. 10).

Conclusion

In balancing individual rights protected under the Canadian Charter of Rights and Freedoms with group rights that provide for religious and cultural accommodations, Alberta and Ontario have become leaders in proactively addressing the rights of minority groups through legislation and programs of choice in public schools. Canada has similarly become a world leader in recognizing collective rights for national minority groups. Quebec occupies a unique position in preserving its distinct francophone identity by protecting the French language and Quebecois culture with legislation. While the discourse of providing increased school choice through decentralized government and more localized accountability at the school level exists in the Canadian context, the extent to which provinces and territories have been willing to accommodate immigrant communities has been mixed. A century and a half after Confederation, it is interesting to note where school choice plays a prominent role in terms of what programs are offered and which local jurisdictions offer them.

In summary, the major historical and political milestones that have influenced and shaped school choice in Canada include the following:

1 Historically, the primary aim of public schooling in English-speaking Canada was to assimilate and unify the nation through education based predominantly on British cultural values, institutions, and practices.
2 Bilingualism within a multicultural framework provided the backdrop for new educational policies regarding heritage-language programs and some religious accommodations in particular jurisdictions

(most notably Jewish schools and non-Catholic Christian schools; Government of Canada, 1965, 1967, 1969a, 1969b). Provisions for these school choice options have been particularly prominent in western Canada but are non-existent in the Atlantic provinces.

3 The Charter of Rights and Freedoms led to both the inclusion of religious practices in public schools (in the case of minority religious cultural practices) and their removal (in the case of the formerly dominant Christian community). It also prompted accommodation for other marginalized groups, such as the LGBT and special needs communities.

4 Educational policymakers in Quebec have been resistant to the principles of multiculturalism. In its place, they have presented interculturalism as a viable framework to guide educational policy, arguing that it ensures all citizens integrate into the dominant francophone culture while requiring that public schools respect diversity.

4

Evolution of School Choice in Canada and the Rise of Parental Rights and Freedoms

In the previous chapters, we examined the philosophical, legal, and historical foundations of school choice policies in Canada, arguing that forms of school choice have been an integral feature of the public education system since the Constitution Act of 1867. During this exploration, we emphasized constitutional developments in Canada that led to the creation of educational arrangements and programs that addressed the identity and cultural needs of national and ethnic minority groups and other minority groups. In this chapter, we turn our attention to how educational movements have shaped the Canadian school landscape to the present day. Although many movements originated in the United States, historical, cultural, and socio-economic differences between the two countries have meant that the impacts of these movements have been quite different in the Canadian context. In addition, because Canadian provinces and territories have control over education, the extent to which school choice programs have been introduced in response to specific reform movements has varied dramatically across the country.

This chapter is divided into two main sections. We begin by turning our attention to the historical evolution of educational reform movements in Canada that emerged in response to shifting sociopolitical and economic realities. We open this discussion by exploring the early formation of public schools in Canada dating back to the middle of the nineteenth century. We examine the rise of the neoliberal market-based reform movement in the 1980s and 1990s, and the more recent educational trends seeking to give parents greater choice in which school their child attends. During our discussion of each reform movement, we provide examples of how each one specifically affected school choice options in Canada. In the second section, we provide a comprehensive overview of the contemporary Canadian school choice landscape. We note provisions for homeschooling, alternative schools, charter schools, and private schools, as well as the introduction of intra-district open enrolment. We discuss the benefits of these options for parents and students and the challenges they create for public education.

Educational Movements That Have Shaped the Canadian School Choice Landscape

The origin of universal, compulsory, free public schooling in English-speaking Canada dates back to the mid-nineteenth century. Before then, children of government officials or members of the military could attend government-aided grammar schools. These schools were for the elite and were not open to children from working-class backgrounds, who had only the option of attending parent- or church-run voluntary schools that provided minimal standards (Sheenan, 1994, p. 44). This situation began to change in provinces and territories outside Quebec through the efforts of early education reformers, the most prominent of whom was Edgerton Ryerson (1803–1882), a Methodist minister and superintendent for education in Ontario, who believed schooling had to be free; open to all children regardless of social status, race, language, or religion; and compulsory. Ryerson regarded public schooling as the great equalizer and the mechanism through which poor children and children of immigrants could rise in social status and contribute to the creation of a better society. Specifically, Ryerson viewed public schooling "as a vehicle of inculcating loyalty and patriotism, fostering social cohesion and self-reliance, and ensuring domestic tranquility" (as quoted in D. Wilson, 1970, p. 215). Based on these educational aims, he produced the *Report on a System of Public Elementary Instruction for Upper Canada, 1846* (Ryerson, 1847), emphasizing the need to create curriculum that would provide students with intellectual and moral development for citizenship, as well as practical knowledge that would prepare them for the workforce.

Seeking to secularize public schools and make them accessible to all, as chief superintendent of education for Upper Canada, Ryerson introduced a number of far-reaching reforms that laid the groundwork for public education across Canada. Overall control of the education system was placed under the authority of the chief superintendent, who

> set standards for the curriculum; supervised the training, inspection and examination of teachers; and oversaw the selection and distribution of

textbooks, through a central depository and press plant which encouraged the publication of works by home-grown authors. Libraries were organized in every school. (Doucet, 2002, p. 1)

To create a centralized, professional organization, Ryerson introduced boards of trustees who reported to district superintendents on a regular basis, worked to raise money, hired teachers, and supplied textbooks (Doucet, 2002). To push for teaching to become a profession, in 1852 Ryerson helped inaugurate the Normal School at St. James Square in Toronto, which housed model schools that provided pre-service teachers with in-class training. To keep in-service teachers up to date on educational developments, Ryerson also helped launch the *Journal of Education for Upper Canada* and set aside two days within the school year in every district for professional conventions.

While many elements of Ryerson's vision of education persisted, in particular the organizing structure of the school system, beginning in the late 1920s educational jurisdictions in Canada began to embrace aspects of the American progressive education movement (Clark, 2004). This new child-centred approach to education emphasized organizing subject matter around students' needs and interests to help them "grow physically, emotionally and spiritually, as well as mentally" (Newland, 1941, as quoted in Clark, 2004, p. 18). Ministries of education throughout Canada designed activity-oriented curricula that promoted cooperation, communication, and the ideals of democratic decision making. This progressive approach to education was introduced under the name of "core curriculum, life adjustment curriculum, or a block program consisting of an integration of social studies with language arts and the humanities" (Clark, 2004, p. 18).

The American progressive education movement can be traced to the work of John Dewey (1859–1952), who believed that education should be aimed at promoting social progress and preparing for participation in democratic life (Dewey, 1916/1966). Aligned with principles of the common school model discussed in Chapter 1, Dewey saw education as a means to socialize children into a common culture with a core set of democratic values in order to enhance social cohesion, form democratic citizens, and forge a democratic society. Dewey argued for forms of education that prioritized science over religion and submitted truly individualistic ideas to those developed in association with other members of society (Godwin & Kemerer, 2002). In seeking to promote democratic life, Dewey felt students needed a form of association that provided opportunity for collective problem-solving through informed discussions and dialogical processes that fostered the greatest amount of participation in determining the common good.

Like Ryerson, Dewey (1916/1966) believed that education could be used as a vehicle to eliminate class differences. Specifically, Dewey felt that public schools could teach creativity and critical deliberation, celebrate diversity by including students from all walks of life, and promote a new kind of individualism. The curriculum served to challenge the values and beliefs that children inherited from their parents. Education was the great equalizer, ensuring equality of opportunity for all students to flourish in a democratic society. For education to accomplish these goals, Dewey believed it was necessary for the state, rather than parents, to have primary control so that a common school experience could transition the child from purely parochial and familial identifications towards broader civic dispositions.

Although the American progressive movement, which drew inspiration from Dewey's (1916/1966) pioneering work in education, was realized in some exemplary school districts and classrooms in Canada, on a systemic level these approaches to education ran counter to a prevailing educational culture that sought to educate dutiful citizens to serve the needs of the expanding industrial economy. Through sorting and streaming students into vocational roles, schools were seen as a way to establish competitive meritocracy. As a result, school choice options were profoundly limited during this time; public schooling was controlled by provincial and territorial educational jurisdictions and designed to achieve cultural uniformity rather than celebrate diversity. Given this, Carson (2006) has asserted that "Canadian curriculum has traditionally been less activist in its ambitions to mould society through schools" (p. 187).

During the 1940s and 1950s, the rise of Cold War anxieties and cultural conservatism in North America wrested education away from progressive reformers and put it into the hands of educational experts concerned with international competitiveness in science and technology. The launching of the Soviet space satellite *Sputnik* in 1957 increased pressure on the West to win the "brain race," resulting in a return to centralized control over schooling and an increased curricular focus on core subjects, such as math, science, and foreign languages. Pedagogically, these educational trends gave rise to the disciplines movement that sought to articulate the modes of inquiry unique to each core subject (Bruner, 1963).

Eventually, the cultural conservatism of the 1950s gave way to more radical and progressive educational mandates during the 1960s. Similar to developments in the United States and the United Kingdom, in Canada the 1960s were marked by intellectual and cultural ferment during which established educational orthodoxies were challenged by new social movements, such as the war on poverty, civil rights, and women's movements. Neoprogressives, also referred to as Romantic Radicals, attacked the public education system for its inability to meet the emotional and developmentally unique needs of individual students, as well as for the way it reproduced a nonegalitarian social order. In response, local school boards, radical "reform" school trustees, and grassroots community groups developed programs to address equity, diversity, poverty, and the needs of disenfranchised groups. As with the earlier progressive education movement, the hallmarks of this period were creativity, innovation, and ways to address the needs of the whole child.

In Ontario, for example, alternative curricular and pedagogical programming emerged in reaction to the dominant educational ideals from the Ryerson era. The *Living and Learning* report (Ontario Ministry of Education, 1968), commonly referred to as the Hall-Dennis Report, was indicative of this changing perspective towards the common school ideal. This report offered 258 recommendations, many of which criticized the authoritarian and regimented nature of Ontarian schools. Among its key observations were the following:

- The curriculum of the future must be child-oriented and must provide opportunities for choice within broadly defined limits.
- There is increasing evidence that children are often better taught in groups centred around interests, and as individuals, than in classes consisting of 30 or 40 pupils. (Ontario Ministry of Education, 1968, pp. 52, 56)

Paralleling developments in other jurisdictions and as a result of this report, schools in Ontario started experimenting with innovative educational approaches, such as child-centred teaching, schools without walls, cooperative learning, and non-graded classes, as well as increased involvement of communities and parents in decision making. Alongside these curricular and pedagogical changes to education, this period also saw the rise of experimental schools, not only as independent schools but also as alternative schools within the Canadian public education system. For instance, in British Columbia, like-minded parents and educators established over 20 alternative schools in the Lower Mainland, Vancouver Island, and the West Kootenays. These schools espoused counterculture idealist world views drawing on elements of pacifism, socialism, and spiritual mysticism (Rothstein, 1999, p. 2). Governed by parent and teacher cooperatives, the curricula varied among schools but in most cases considered personal growth, unrestrained exploration, and community building equally important as academic learning (Rothstein, 1999, p. 2).

In Toronto in 1966, a group of school activists founded Everdale Place, Canada's first free school. They published an influential, alternative political magazine called *This Magazine Is About Schools*, challenging the political left in Canada to consider grassroots initiatives in response to entrenched mainstream schools in Ontario (Murnaghan, 2009, p. 37). In 1972, the Alpha Alternative School continued this trend by opening an alternative public schooling option based on democratic principles. Drawing on the ideals of student-centred, progressive education, the school encouraged active engagement, critical-thinking skills, community-based teaching opportunities, and the recognition "that all children are unique and develop differently and at different rates" (Alpha Alternative School, 2015, para. 3). Another notable example of a Canadian parent-initiated alternative school established in the early 1970s is the Saturday School in Calgary, which emphasized aesthetic education, integration of curriculum, and a cooperative and democratic school community (Rothstein, 1999, p. 10). Other schools that were part of this educational trend included the Greenhouse School in Regina and St. Norbert's Community School in Winnipeg.

As outlined in Chapter 3, the school choice movement during the early 1970s also led to the introduction of heritage-language immersion programs for some groups – especially in western Canada. In addition, because there were no provisions for religious schools that were not Roman Catholic in most public education systems, some school boards in western Canada allowed some formerly private schools to move into the public system. This was the case in Edmonton, for example, where the Talmud Torah School joined the Edmonton Public School Board in 1975 as a Hebrew bilingual school (A. Taylor & Mackay, 2008). However, by the latter part of the 1970s, provisions for alternative schooling in Canada began to shift towards providing spaces for "disaffected young people left over from the volatile 1960s [to] learn basic academic skills in an accepting and unpressured environment, meanwhile developing personal characteristics that would help them function more effectively in society" (Rothstein, 1999, p. 2).

The 1980s signalled an end to the halcyon days of the 1960s and 1970s curricular innovation, experimentation, and high trust in professional educators. The global recession of the late 1970s and early 1980s, along with new international trade agreements aimed at reducing economic protectionism, fuelled anxiety among middle-class parents that current models of education were not adequately preparing their children for new global and hyper-competitive economic realities. The newly emerging knowledge-based economy signalled that intellectual capital had currency, and effort and ability alone were insufficient to ensure career advancement through the labour market. Not only did this increase the demand for higher education, but it also created demand among parents to provide enhanced educational opportunities for their children at the elementary and secondary school levels. A growing number of parents believed that the educational success of their children was too important to be left to monolithic, one-size-fits-all education systems that played to the lowest common denominator. Instead, they sought to provide their children with a competitive advantage through independent or specialist schools and private tutorial services.

The move towards educational reform that would make students more economically competitive was also fuelled by the election of right-wing governments both federally and in some provinces that drew on laissez-faire market principles in an effort to counter an educational agenda that they felt reflected a rising tide of public sector mediocrity. Politicians accused schools of being "out of touch" and "behind the times" and unable to reform themselves to meet the new economic needs of a globalizing world. These developments in Canada were additionally influenced by American educational reformers who claimed schools had lost sight of the basic purpose of education and were no longer able to meet the high expectations and disciplined effort necessary to attain higher student achievement (Belfield & Levin, 2002; Chubb & Moe, 1990; Coulson, 2009; Hess, 2009; Merrifield, 2008; Ouchi, 2003). This educational reform movement was mirrored internationally in reports and legislation, including *A Nation at Risk* (National Commission on Excellence in Education, 1983) and the No Child Left Behind Act of 2001 in the United States, as well as the White Paper *Excellence in Schools* (Department for Education, Gov.UK, 1997) in the United Kingdom.

Within the Canadian context, the report *Knowledge Matters: Skills and Learning for Canadians* (Government of Canada, Human Resource Development Canada, 2002), as well as the policy document *Achieving Excellence: Investing in People, Knowledge and Opportunity* (Government of Canada, Industry Canada, 2002), encouraged provincial and territorial ministries of education to increase the levels of educational attainment and vocational skill training, among other reforms. These sentiments were echoed by influential think tanks and special interest groups, such as the Society for the Advancement of Excellence in Education, the Fraser Institute, Canada West Foundation, and the C.D. Howe Institute. These largely right-wing organizations argued that overly bureaucratic forms of administration and powerful teacher unions had created a public education system unresponsive to the demands of the new global economy. They called for market-based education reform that would eliminate barriers to parental choice and expand competition to make the system more responsive, effective, and efficient (Guillemette, 2007; Hepburn, 2001; Holmes, 1998; Lawton, Freedman, & Robertson, 1995).

Because of these developments, the late 1980s and early 1990s were marked by the rise of neoliberal-inspired education reforms that focused on restructuring public schools to ensure the social and economic prosperity of the nation. These changes led some educational jurisdictions in Canada to adopt an educational agenda that enabled various types of school choice. Alberta was the most responsive to this educational reform agenda, evidenced by the accountability measures introduced, including quality assurance frameworks (provincial achievement testing in grades 6 and 9, and diploma exams for grade 12) and the introduction of choice initiatives that included provisions for charter schools, partial funding for accredited private schools, and support for homeschooling.

While calls for reforms based on accountability, choice, and competition have not disappeared, educational developments of the early twenty-first century reflect demands for new models of teaching and learning that better engage learners and provide them with the competencies to become more innovative and creative. Task forces have produced reports to provide a new vision for public education nationally (Boudreault et al., 2013; Canadians for 21st Century Learning & Innovation, 2012; Employment and Social Development Canada, 2014; Partnership for 21st Century Skills, n.d.) and provincially in British Columbia (British Columbia Ministry of Education, 2015), Alberta (Alberta Education, 2011b), Ontario (Fullan, 2013; Ontario Ministry of Education, 2014), Quebec (Quebec Ministry of Education, 2001, 2004), and New Brunswick (New Brunswick Department of Education, 2010). These frameworks share a common focus on foundational learning in literacy, numeracy, and science, as well as core competencies, such as critical thinking, innovation, digital literacy, and creativity. Within the context of digitally enhanced learning environments, educators are required to leverage the power of digital networks to personalize and tailor courses to suit students' learning preferences. Educators have also been called on to engage learners in more self-directed learning while providing greater opportunities for teamwork and collaboration.

As part of this educational vision, students have more choice and responsibility in their learning with diminished reliance on transmission models of teaching that require set classes in schools. Constructivist, inquiry-based learning has been encouraged, with new forms of assessment and less emphasis on standardized testing and grades. Alberta Education's (2010) *Inspiring Education* is emblematic of this shift in thinking. By fostering intellectual engagement, an entrepreneurial spirit, and the dispositions of ethical citizenship, *Inspiring Education* advocates a vision of education in which students develop competencies through a process of inquiry and discovery. Students collaborate to create new knowledge while also learning how to "think critically and creatively, and how to make discoveries – through inquiry, reflection, exploration, experimentation, and trial and error" (Alberta Education, 2010, p. 19).

This shift in thinking has not been without its detractors. Sceptics view this approach to learning as a return to the romantic progressivism of the 1960s. Some parent groups and high-profile national columnists have called for the preservation of teacher-guided, knowledge-based education with clear standards and measures of student achievement outcomes (Alphonso & Maki, 2014; Trans-Davies, 2014; Wente, 2014). Citing the effectiveness of traditional approaches to math that rely on rote learning, for example, Trans-Davies (2014) organized a petition demanding that Alberta Education return to traditional approaches to education. She wrote:

> It is, therefore, a great injustice not only to our children, but to all children around the world when the bureaucrats here, in this land of opportunities, are squandering our children's right to a good education in their attempt to appear innovative even as they break down the valuable roles of a teacher and the school in our children's education. (Trans-Davies, 2014, para. 8)

By October 2014, Trans-Davies's petition had garnered over 10,000 signatures, including from people outside Alberta ("Petition Calls," 2014). With this level of opposition, Alberta Education's vision as outlined in *Inspiring Education* is uncertain. Given these reactionary responses to the most recent trends in education, emerging approaches may provide the impetus for new forms of schooling and the expansion of choice options. Specifically, trends in education seem to be moving towards technology-enhanced delivery, the creation of a wider variety of specialty schools within public school boards, additional online learning options, open catchment programs, partial funding for independent schools, and increased support for homeschooling.

Contemporary School Choice Landscape

The provinces and territories operate on a broad spectrum for providing and funding school choice options and accommodating parents' desire for control in determining the education for their children that reflects their family values and the aspirations they hold for their children. At one end of the spectrum, Alberta offers the most school choice options and is the only jurisdiction with charter schools. At the other end, the Atlantic provinces and three territories offer the fewest options. Beyond the school choice options discussed in Chapter 2 that include provisions for heritage-language and faith-based schools, Table 4 provides a comparative snapshot of three other schooling opportunities available in Canada. We discuss each of these school choice options in detail.

Homeschooling

Perhaps the most contentious domain of school choice occurs when parents express their rights and preferences by removing their children from school and educating them at home. At issue is the degree of freedom parents should have regarding the education of their children, which stands in relation to the responsibility of the state in defining terms for the provision and supervision of education. Homeschooling raises questions concerning the right of the state to protect children's interests and rights to develop independent judgment, self-determination, and competency for liberal citizenship (Thiessen, 2001, p. 77).

Homeschooling pioneers in North America can be traced to two vastly different groups: religious fundamentalists and experimental-type John Holt–inspired "unschoolers." Religious fundamentalists generally homeschool their children by following a curriculum infused with religious values, focusing on the basics, and promoting the authority of the family. Drawing on church-based organizations, Christian homeschools have a highly developed network of families, support groups, and access to educational materials (Davies & Aurini, 2003, p. 64). In contrast, "unschooling" is a movement inspired by John Holt, who in the 1960s encouraged parents to teach their own children in natural (home) settings, letting

Table 4. School Choice in Canada

Province or territory	Homeschooling	Independent/ private schools	Open enrolment in public systems
British Columbia	No funding support	35%–50% funded	Province-wide open enrolment.
Alberta[a]	$1641 per student per year	60%–70% funded	Open enrolment allowed but exact rules are determined at the school board level. Generally, transportation costs are not covered.
Saskatchewan	Up to $1000 per student per year	50%–80% funded	No open enrolment policy.
Manitoba	No funding support	50% funded	Provincial authorization for open enrolment; some conditions apply.
Ontario	No funding support	No provincial funding	Province offers conditional open enrolment for distance and geographic considerations in Schools Act. Additional considerations are determined at the district/board level.
Quebec	No funding support	Up to 60% funded	Provincially authorized open enrolment within school districts.
New Brunswick	No funding support	No provincial funding	No open enrolment; student placement determined by school district with appeal process.
Nova Scotia	No funding support	No provincial funding	No provincial open enrolment policy. Issue is determined at board level.
Prince Edward Island	No funding support	No provincial funding	No open enrolment; student placement determined by school district.
Newfoundland & Labrador	No funding support	No provincial funding	No open enrolment.
Yukon, Northwest Territories, Nunavut	No funding support	No extra funding	No open enrolment.

Source: Adapted from J. Clemens, M. Palacios, J. Loyer, & F. Fathers, *Measuring Choice and Competition in Canadian Education: An Update on School Choice in Canada*, 2014, pp. 4–5. Copyright 2014 by the Barbara Mitchell Centre for Improvement in Education (Fraser Institute).

[a] Alberta also offers charter school options, the only province to do so.

the innate curiosity of the child, rather than a prescribed curriculum, direct learning. Many families who adopted an unschooling approach to educate their children embraced a more free-spirited and independent alternative lifestyle that "rejected structured materialism and career orientations of the mainstream" (Davies & Aurini, 2003, p. 64). Pockets of parents following this approach exist in various communities across Canada, particularly in British Columbia's West Kootenays and on Vancouver Island. In the 1960s, a significant number of young Americans left their country for political reasons and took up alternative lifestyles in these areas (Rothstein, 1999).

Before the 1960s, poor access to education facilities because of geographic distance, physical or mental disability, or religious conviction were central reasons Canadian parents educated their children at home. More recently, new subgroups of homeschoolers have emerged with different goals, ranging from "nurturing minority identities to meeting special educational needs, to simply seeking a superior form of education" (Aurini & Davies, 2005, p. 462). Canadian parents generally choose to homeschool their children because of dissatisfaction with the public education system in terms of a perceived lack of focus on academic performance and discipline, and concern regarding a physically and emotionally safe learning environment (Basham & Hepburn, 2001). Online resources and courses, public virtual schools, and independent education services provide support for students and families choosing blended approaches to schooling. Where private education is too costly for a family, homeschooling can be the most viable option, providing the opportunity to impart a particular set of values consistent with family child-rearing beliefs and lifestyle.

Supporters of homeschooling are adamant that parents are in a better position than the state to judge the educational needs of their children. They believe that parents should have primary responsibility for deciding how their children should be educated. This stance is reflected in a statement from the Coalition of Independent Homeschoolers:

> We aren't so interested in the approval or endorsement of government agencies or educational organizations, and we tend to be sceptical about accepting funds or aid from these sources and even about making use of the services they may be interested in offering to us. (quoted in Davies & Aurini, 2008, p. 71)

Agreement exists among policymakers, however, that some forms of restriction and supervision are necessary to ensure the best interests of children are served (Merry & Karsten, 2010, p. 499).

The major objections to homeschooling are similar to those for private schools: it aggravates social inequality, perpetuates counterculture movements, and interferes with the well-being and interests of children. The possibility also exists that this form of schooling serves undemocratic, sometimes elitist, often backward, and divisive interests (Goodenow, 1988). A particular concern is that students who attend homeschooling forgo exposure to perspectives other than those of their family and close community surroundings. They have limited exposure to diverse ideas and individuals that are part of the larger pluralist society (Reich, 2002a). This negative idea is exacerbated by an increasing subset of homeschooled children coming from conservative religious families (Kunzman, 2010).

Canada has seen an increase in homeschooling since the 1970s, when just 2000 children were homeschooled (Basham & Hepburn, 2001). By the 1990s, "the respective provincial ministries of education put the number of homeschooled children at 17,523, or 0.4% of total student enrolment – a 776% increase over just 18 years. Today, some estimates put the number of homeschooled students in Canada as high as 80,000" (Basham & Hepburn, 2001, p. 6). A more recent study by Van Pelt (2015) indicates 23,992 children are homeschooled in Canada, still representing only 0.4% of total student enrolment. Davies and Aurini (2003) have noted the difficulty in determining an accurate number because of a lack of uniform regulations for tracking homeschooled students. For example, some families fail to register their children with local authorities, move their children between public or private schools and the homeschool, or register their children part-time for some courses in public or private schools. As a result, under-reporting of the number of homeschooled students in Canada is likely. Aurini and Davies (2005) noted that homeschooling is enjoying increased legitimacy within the school choice movement; however, their findings indicate that most parents who assert their right to choose do not espouse market ideology. Instead, the majority are engaged in a culture of intensive parenting that focuses on cultivating the unique needs of their child.

Homeschooling is legal in all provinces and territories. At a minimum, parents are required to comply with provincial and territorial school law. Among the provinces, Alberta, as a leader in provisions for choice, provides the most funding to families for homeschooling. Parents in Alberta are required to notify a school board or accredited private school of their intent to homeschool their children and agree to have their children's performance evaluated twice a year. According to Alberta Education's (2006) *Home Education Regulations,*

Associate school boards and associate private schools will continue to evaluate the performance of home-educated students based on the education programs planned and provided by parents. Home-educated students will continue to be visited at least twice each year by a teacher from the associate school board or associate private school. These teachers will measure progress by reviewing samples of the students' work and by observing students while they perform learning tasks. Information gathered at these visits will be shared with parents. (Strengthening Home Education section, para. 2)

With recent changes to legislation in Saskatchewan, school districts can provide up to $1000 per student for homeschooling for children registered with the local school board. The funding amount varies among school jurisdictions (Van Pelt, 2015).

In contrast, Ontario provides no funding but recognizes homeschooling as a viable alternative to public education, allowing parents to choose educational experiences appropriate to their family. Parents in Ontario who want to homeschool their children are not required to follow the traditional curriculum or seek approval from provincial school inspectors; they simply need to notify the school board of their intent to homeschool (Davies & Aurini, 2008, p. 66).

Independent schools

Along with the public school system, every jurisdiction in Canada has an independent school system that operates as a distinct entity outside the public system. Canada has a long history of traditional (academically focused) and religious private schools, mainly in Ontario, British Columbia, and Quebec – some of which are boarding schools and single-gender schools that serve affluent families who can afford the tuition and expenses. More recently, independent schools geared towards the aspirations of middle-class parents have emerged. They include schools distinguished by their philosophical orientation to education (Montessori, Waldorf, Reggio Emillia), as well as specialty schools that cater to particular segments of students with programming to accommodate the pursuit of special activities (sports, arts, military). The number of independent schools in Canada that cater to online learning to supplement or replace traditional school-based instruction and homeschooling has also increased.

Advocates of independent schools uphold the liberty of parents to choose how their children are educated. Independent schools are deemed attractive because they provide students with access to social networks of families and alumni; enriched curriculum focused on the cultivation of dispositions, knowledge, and skills for success in life; and enhanced consideration for admission to some postsecondary institutions. However, it is noteworthy that not all independent schools in Canada would be categorized as elite preparatory schools catering to wealthy families. Independent schools also share the common feature of providing parents with choice in the education and socialization of their children in homogeneous communities of like-minded parents, supported by educators who, at least in principle, believe in the culture, pedagogical orientation, and overall mission of the school.

Those against the public provisioning of money for independent schools have voiced concerns regarding the emergence of unregulated independent schools and the unchecked risk factors parents assume in choosing these schools for their children. They argue these schools exacerbate inequalities along socio-economic lines because only a small sector of families can afford the tuition and associated expenses. Specifically, socio-economically advantaged parents who send their children to private or independent schools with selective admission policies are able to use their added resources to maintain their child's competitive edge over other children and increase their life opportunities. However, advocates of independent schools counter that in addition to independent school tuition fees, parents also pay taxes to support public education; it is therefore unreasonable to hold parents responsible for making society more equal. They hold the public system of education accountable for failing to address issues of equity and diversity. They argue school districts have the pooled resources available, if they wanted, to work on behalf of parents who lack the resources or sociocultural capital to intervene effectively for their children (Fried, 1998).

Regulatory frameworks for independent schools vary among jurisdictions, with heavy regulation in Quebec and few regulations in Ontario. For example, the Ontario Education Act defines a private school as

> an institution at which instruction is provided at any time between the hours of 9 am and 4 pm on any school day for five or more pupils who are of or over compulsory school age in any of the elementary or secondary school courses of study. (as quoted in Allison & Van Pelt, 2012, pp. 104–105)

Unregulated schools in Ontario are not required to hire certified teachers or follow the provincial program of studies. Many of the newer independent schools of this nature serve niche markets that keep enrolment low, focus on specialized pedagogy, and provide intimate, personalized learning environments for their students.

Funding levels for independent schools vary across Canada. British Columbia, Alberta, Saskatchewan, Manitoba, and Quebec provide public funding for independent schools. Funding levels for independent schools in these provinces range from a low of 35%–50% in British Columbia to a high of up to 80% in Saskatchewan (Clemens et al., 2014, pp. 25–26). Within these provinces, independent schools must adhere to minimum requirements, such as following the provincially approved curriculum or program of studies. In some provinces, meeting a set criteria serves as a form of accreditation, and unaccredited schools receive no funding. Notably, Ontario, the Atlantic provinces, and the territories provide no funding for independent schools; therefore, independent schools in these provinces and territories enjoy a relative degree of autonomy from provincial or territorial regulations compared with those in jurisdictions that do provide funding.

The percentage of the total student population attending independent schools varies by province, with Quebec (12.5%) and British Columbia (12.1%) having the highest enrolment, and New Brunswick (0.9%) and Prince Edward Island (0.9%) having the lowest (Clemens et al., 2014, p. 26). Clemens et al. (2014, p. 26) observed that while Ontario does not provide funding for independent schools, it has a higher percentage of students enrolled in these schools (5.1%) than Alberta (4.6%) and Saskatchewan (1.0%), two provinces that provide funding (see Table 5). The Association of Independent Schools and Colleges in Alberta (2008) estimated that between 2005 and 2009, 5460 formerly independent students in grades 1 to 12 shifted to public student status. They attributed this to independent schools that have elected to become alternative programs and operate under the authority of public school boards to receive full provincial funding for their students.

Charter schools

Currently, the charter school movement has taken hold only in Alberta. With a series of right-wing parties elected without interruption for almost 80 years, Alberta has been long considered the most conservative province in Canada. This political stability has permitted the Progressive Conservative Party, which was in power from 1971 to 2015, to adopt more neoliberal approaches to educational reform through parental choice and market mechanisms in the public education system than other

Table 5. Independent School Enrolment, 2009–2010

Province	Number of students	Percentage of total enrolment
British Columbia	69,455	12.1
Alberta	27,426	4.6
Saskatchewan	1,593	1.0
Manitoba	14,172	7.4
Ontario	111,168	5.1
Quebec	125,913	12.5
New Brunswick	990	0.9
Nova Scotia	2,949	2.2
Prince Edward Island	206	0.9
Newfoundland & Labrador	830	1.2

Source: Adapted from J. Clemens, M. Palacios, J. Loyer, & F. Fathers, *Measuring Choice and Competition in Canadian Education: An Update on School Choice in Canada*, 2014, p. 26. Copyright 2014 by the Barbara Mitchell Centre for Improvement in Education (Fraser Institute).

educational jurisdictions in Canada. As part of these developments, in 1994 the government of Alberta passed legislation to establish charter schools. These schools were introduced as an "addition to the public education system" (Alberta Education, 2011a, p. 1) and as sites of innovation that would "complement the educational services provided by the local public system [and provide the] ... opportunity for successful educational practices to be recognized and adopted by other public schools for the benefit of more students" (Alberta Education, 2011a, p. 1).

Charter school legislation was introduced shortly after the national debate regarding the role of education in enhancing Canada's ability to compete in a global marketplace (Corporate Higher-Learning Forum, 1990; Economic Council of Canada, 1992; Steering Group on Prosperity, 1992). The outcome of these debates was a call by various national agencies for ministries of education across Canada to establish environments that encouraged individuals to take greater responsibility for their children's learning, schools to define their mission and articulate their methods for attaining it, and stakeholders to assume responsibility for results (Corporate Higher-Learning Forum, 1990). These agencies advocated that "clients" should be able to choose the institution that best satisfied their needs and aspirations and that there be real differences among institutions.

Given this broader context, the Alberta government responded by positioning education as a commodity in the marketplace. Charter schools were heralded as a vehicle to advance the goals of accountability, efficiency, and performance, and to empower parents and other members of the community to have more direct involvement at the school level (Bosetti, 1998b). Along with charter school legislation, the Alberta government increased funding to private schools; reduced overall funding to education by 12%; expanded provincial standardized testing programs to grades 3, 6, and 9; maintained grade 12 diploma examinations; promoted site-based management as the preferred model of school management; required parent-based school councils; and consolidated school boards from 141 to 68 (Bruce & Schwartz, 1997). The desired outcome was a public education system that was goal oriented, service oriented, and responsive to market forces (Bosetti, 2000).

In Alberta, charter schools are autonomous, non-profit, public entities organized by like-minded parents and educators to provide choices in educational philosophy, mission, or delivery, as well as governance and organization. They are granted flexibility and considerable autonomy to implement these innovative or enhanced educational services to improve student learning in some measurable way. As sites of innovation, they have increased responsibility for research and dissemination of effective practices. Given these parameters, charter schools cannot have a religious affiliation or charge tuition fees.

Like the public schools, charter schools hire certified teachers; however, their teachers are non-unionized, do not engage in collective bargaining, and are not full members of the Alberta Teachers' Association. Teachers are required to follow the provincially mandated program of study, and students participate in provincial standardized achievement and diploma examinations. Charter schools manage their own funding, are eligible for the same per-pupil grants as public schools, and submit an annual report on their performance. They operate on a five-year contract, as defined by the terms of their charter, which is approved and monitored by the Minister of Education. At the time of renewal, an external evaluation is conducted to determine whether the charter school has complied with its legal and financial requirements, has fulfilled its charter objectives, and has demonstrated parental and community support. Based on this assessment, renewal of the charter may or may not be recommended. To date, only two charter schools have been closed.

The Ministry of Education, with an initial cap of 15 schools, has carefully managed the growth of charter schools in Alberta. Of the 15 charter schools, 11 are located in urban settings and 4 are in rural or semirural locations (Ritchie, 2010); approximately 8100 students are enrolled (Lukaszuk, 2012). Charter schools' success in creating market pressure through choice and competition is evident in student demand, waiting lists for admission, and multiple campus sites, challenging public schools to be more responsive to diverse student needs by offering more programs of choice. For most charter schools established in urban areas, local public school boards have adopted a version of their charters as alternative programs in their school system. Recent amendments to the Charter School Regulations (Government of Alberta, 2012) have lifted the cap on charter schools and addressed concerns regarding the long-term viability of established charter schools. Charter schools meeting specific criteria can apply for a 15-year charter renewal and an increase in their enrolment cap; to be successful, the charter school must demonstrate research-informed practice, strong student achievement, continuous improvement, and community engagement.

Overall, charter schools have provided enhanced student learning outcomes as compared to similar schools and similar students enrolled in other jurisdictions (Government of Alberta, 2011). In a recent study, Johnson (2013) identified Alberta's best schools by using student results on provincial achievement tests in math, reading, science, and social studies in grades 3, 6, and 9. In his analysis, he compared students from public, private, and charter schools on an "apples-to-apples" basis, where he controlled for observed student background (socio-economic status) and indicated "good" schools where principals, teachers, and staff were having a noticeably positive impact on student performance. His study of 800 schools revealed a disproportionate number of private and charter schools ranking in the upper echelons, with the gap between charter schools and all other schools large and consistent across all three grades. Johnson reasoned this discrepancy might be attributed to charter schools selecting the best students and rejecting weaker applicants, hiring stronger teachers, and crafting their mandates to match the interests of families and teachers who choose these schools, thereby producing better results.

Perhaps the biggest concern surrounding the introduction of choice mechanisms, such as charter schools, into public education is that market mechanisms, rather than political debate, determine the goals and values of education. In contrast, in line with critiques of independent schools, criticisms of charter schools point to the creation of a two-tiered system of education where children from disadvantaged families not in the position to engage in educational markets are left behind in their neighbourhood schools. As specialist schools with particular mandates, charter schools are thought to have a creaming effect by attracting and selecting students who fit their mandate, creating homogenous value communities and contributing to the fragmentation of society. However, it is arguable as to whether this is the case in Alberta, where charter schools address marginalized groups, such as at-risk youth (Boyle Street Education Centre), children for whom English is a second language (Almadina Language Charter Academy), and Indigenous children (Mother Earth's Children's Charter School).

The first generation of charter schools has been an effective engine in driving the public education system to provide more choice and voice for parents. In a recent concept paper, the Alberta government held out the vision for the second generation of charter schools as catalysts for critical thinking about innovations in teaching and learning, and incubators to fine-tune ideas or concepts into educational experiences that advance student success (Alberta Education, 2009). Charter mandates should thus include a stronger research agenda in the future:

> Each charter could define the scope of the ideas to be explored and the scope of the foundational requirements in basic education, such as alternative forms of the programs of study, different approaches to staffing, other ways to evaluate student success and alternative forms of funding. (Alberta Education, 2009, p. 2)

Parents, teachers, school administrators, and students would choose charter schools with the knowledge of their mandate to be innovative, and children would be involved in research initiatives to enhance education and student success.

Alternative schools (programs) and open enrolment policies

School choice options within school districts can take the form of specialized schools, alternative schools, or alternative programs. These alternative schools offer a unique learning environment, philosophical orientation, or curriculum that diverges from the traditional or mainstream program.

Sometimes referred to as magnet schools or academies, they are designed to provide choice for families to select programs best suited to the learning preferences and aptitudes of their children.

These programs attract students from across the district, and in some cases admission is competitive and selective (see Table 4, School Choice in Canada). Because students in the public system are assigned to a designated school for tracking and planning purposes, various rules and restrictions are used for admission to alternative schools. Districts offering programs of choice (British Columbia, Alberta, Manitoba, Ontario, and Quebec) usually adopt open boundary attendance policies that enable parents to choose schools outside their catchment area. Parents may be required to cover transportation costs, the child must meet admission requirements, and the school must have room to accommodate the student. High-demand alternative schools with waiting lists often employ a lottery system for admission.

As discussed in the previous section on educational movements in Canada, alternative schools have had a robust history in Canada, reflective of the sociocultural and political context of different historical periods. The majority of alternative schools were created as independent schools by grassroots movements organized by parents and educators dissatisfied with the status quo of the dominant public education system. More recently, urban school boards in most parts of Canada have become more responsive to demands from parents and marginalized groups for alternative education programs to address the diverse needs and interests of these students (Gaskell & Levin, 2012).

Aside from a focus on student achievement, school boards use alternative education programs strategically for a range of purposes. These include helping schools "[to respond] to emerging unmet learning needs, to foster innovation, to test new pedagogical practices, and to renew inner city neighbourhoods where school buildings have excess space" (Maguire, 2006, p. vi), as well as to provide mechanisms for accountability and efficiency, where "success indicators of student achievement, enrolment, demand, and parent satisfaction are consistently monitored" (Maguire, 2006, p. vi). For example, in British Columbia, alternative education programs focus on addressing "educational, social and emotional issues for students whose needs are not being met in a traditional school program. An alternate education program provides its support through differentiated instruction, specialized program delivery and enhanced counselling services based on students' needs" (British Columbia Ministry of Education, 2009, para. 1). This meeting of needs is also the case in

Ontario, where alternative schools "provide an option for students who have educational needs that cannot be met in their existing schools, and/or to respond to needs expressed in the community" (Ontario Ministry of Education, 2011, p. 74). Specialized schools focus on "the arts, business studies, the environment, languages, pure and applied sciences, or technological education" (Ontario Ministry of Education, 2011, p. 74).

The Edmonton Public School Board has been one of the most responsive school districts in Canada, achieving both national and international recognition for its wide variety of school choice programs in place since 1974. Its philosophy states:

> We believe that the "one size fits all" model of education is no longer appropriate in today's rapidly evolving society. Children have different learning styles and some achieve better in certain environments. Edmonton Public Schools is making a strong statement about our ability to address and meet the changing needs of students. (Edmonton Public School Board, 2012, para. 4)

More than 40 years ago the Edmonton Public School Board created a revolutionary open boundary system that allowed parents and students to pursue educational programming in a learning environment of their choice (Edmonton Public School Board, 1974). Since choice is the foundation of the school district's approach to education, it has devoted considerable resources to guiding parents through the decision-making process of finding and choosing an appropriate school. It has developed an online Find a School toolkit that includes a quick guide to planning a child's education, a district map of schools and listings, open house events, and school websites with demographic information on the student population, student achievement results on provincial exams, transportation costs, budget, and extracurricular activities. The Edmonton Public School Board, like other school boards in Canada, has developed alternative programs to provide choice to parents and to accommodate the particular learning needs, preferences, and aptitudes of children with the aim of enhanced student achievement and success.

While provisions for alternative programs have been embraced by some school districts in Canada, this form of school choice is not without its critics. Many of the criticisms centre on issues of equity and whether alternative programs ensure fair admission policies, as well as adequate information and support for parents to make informed decisions about the options available to them. Critics argue that provisions for alternative

schools often fail to ensure that lower-income families and hard-to-educate students are provided the necessary support to engage in educational choice that would lead to equitable and fair access to programs
and schools. There are also issues related to fair access in terms of the
extra transportation costs often associated with having children attend
alternative schools. Some critics fear that these schools could lead to the
segregation of students along ability, socio-economic, religious, or ethnic lines. These critics hold to the belief that the common school ideal,
where the vast majority of students attend a standard public school designated by their neighbourhood, can best accommodate the educational
needs of individuals and the greater society.

Conclusion

In this chapter, we have focused on the historical, sociocultural, and
educational movements that influenced the terrain of school choice in
Canada. Canada has a robust history of accommodation within the public education system for social diversity. However, some provinces have
been more proactive in creating policies and funding to support a range
of choices for parents. The following is a summary of the key themes in
this chapter.

1 While legislation to support alternative forms of schooling varies
across Canada, all parents in Canada have the right to homeschool
their children and to access private or independent schools. In some
provinces, school boards have well-established alternative programs
that offer choice to families, and in Alberta, there are public charter
schools. Parents who decide to exercise school choice opportunities
have largely done so based on their dissatisfaction with the forms
of education offered by the mainstream public education system.
2 Homeschooling is perhaps the most extreme example of alternative
schooling, where parents can have the most control over the education and socialization of their children by removing them from
the public education system. In contrast, private and independent
schools are options available for parents who can afford the tuition
fees and have children who meet the specific admission standards.
3 Responses to school choice provisions within the publically funded
school system include alternative programs, which often go hand
in hand with open enrolment boundaries within school districts.
In these cases, school boards offer programs to respond to students'

diverse interests and learning needs, and offer choices in the philosophical or pedagogical orientation of the education provided. These schools still foster a form of common schooling within the public system but provide alternatives to the comprehensive neighbourhood school.

4 Charter schools in Alberta reflect market-based approaches to educational reform by providing competition in the public education system and challenge the monopoly of teacher unions and school boards on the governance and administration of public education.

5 A central criticism of school choice is that market mechanisms, rather than political debate, determine the goals and values of education. Other concerns relate to issues of equity, access, and social cohesion. Schools of choice cater to middle-class families with the resources to navigate the system and access their school of choice. Specialist programs have a creaming effect in attracting students with particular attributes and aptitudes, leaving behind the hard-to-educate and children from marginalized groups. In some cases, alternative programs cater to marginalized and vulnerable students, segregating them from the mainstream. This division creates a two-tiered education system and further fragments society.

5

School Choice as Concerted Cultivation: Middle-Class Anxiety and Advantage

In this chapter, we turn to a deeper investigation of the sociocultural and psychological factors that influence how parents engage in school choice, the effects of social class in their choice-seeking behaviour, and the limitations of school choice policy in achieving equality of opportunity for children. We begin with a critical analysis of the concept of meritocracy and the role of schooling in mitigating inequality. Drawing on Canadian-based research, we examine key factors that limit socio-economically disadvantaged families from engaging in educational markets and their children from participating in and benefiting from many of the programs of choice offered by school districts. We discuss these factors in three parts: (1) parents as active choosers – the significance of habitus, agency, and forms of rationality in choosing schools; (2) middle-class anxiety, school choice, and intensive forms of parenting that alter relations with public school educators as parents seek not only to support but also to advocate for advantages for their child; and (3) the hidden costs in accessing programs of choice. We look at research conducted in Alberta to illustrate how these factors play out (D. Ball, 2007; Bosetti, 2000, 2004; Bosetti & Pyryt, 2007; Gereluk, 2006; A. Taylor & Mackay, 2008).

Dispelling the Myth of the Meritocratic Society

The recent expansion of school choice options offered from a variety of service providers has created market incentives for public schools to respond to parental demands for more choice in programs for their children and to address students' learning needs and preferences. Public pressure and government accountability schemes compel schools to demonstrate improved outcomes in terms of student achievement, engagement, and retention. Despite these initiatives, provisions for school choice have been criticized for their inability to secure equality of opportunity in education (Arneson, 1999; Tooley, 2000; J. Wilson, 1991) or effectively target lower-socio-economic families whose children could benefit from these programs (S. Ball, 2003; Ben-Porath, 2009). Part of the challenge is that public education is based on the assumption that Canada is a meritocratic society. Specifically, the ideals of a democratic society aim to reduce societal inequalities by providing individuals with opportunities to increase their social mobility through their natural talents and hard work. Although plenty of evidence shows that social class differences are marked and defined throughout Canadian society, the narrative played out in the political rhetoric that individuals can change their economic circumstance through the quality and quantity of education received, and the degree of effort in their future (usually economic) endeavours. Public education, based on these principles of meritocracy, is viewed as one of the primary equalizers for creating a more level playing field and as a vehicle for individuals to attain the skills, disposition, and credentials necessary to achieve employability and a level of income that enhances their social status and life chances.

These concepts of education-based meritocracy and life chances merit further exploration. The idea of meritocracy was originally proposed by Young (1958) to describe the relationship between educational achievement and the resulting social position that individuals attain; he described merit as IQ plus effort.[1] Given equality of opportunity, a system of stratification or sorting emerges based on individual attainment of educational credentials, determined by ability and effort, which subsequently determines the acquisition of economic opportunity and status (Wright, 2008, p. 343). The prime criterion of social selection becomes educated talent, demonstrated through achievement of formal qualifications and credentials, rather than ascribed because of birth and family

---

1 Young's 1958 book, *The Rise of Meritocracy* – a social fantasy and dystopia – was written as a warning to British society. He was concerned the postwar government was using the Education Act of 1944 with the intent of providing "education for all" as an instrumental device to sort children based on merit into different educational streams (e.g., academic, technical, and general). Educational achievement as measured by success on examinations and attainment of credentials provided access to different "grades" of employment and levels of reward. He feared this would contribute to a new form of social stratification, with little improvement of the class-based society of Britain (Goldthorpe & Jackson, 2008, p. 93).

status. Simply put, schools can positively affect a person's future economic opportunities.

Life chances are related to normative issues of equality of opportunity, which in turn are related to material standards of living. Inequality is defined by deficient relationships to income-generating resources or assets, which constitute forms of capital, such as intellectual (knowledge and ability), economic (money), social (wealth, power, status), and cultural (family background, norms, values, and beliefs), that people use to achieve things considered to be culturally important. Wright (2008) questioned the extent to which "children born into different families of different economic standings have equal opportunities to succeed in life [and achieve in the public education system]" (p. 331). He presented the simple formula, "What you have determines what you get" (Wright, 2008, p. 331).

This starting premise – that meritocracy, in and of itself, can mitigate social and economic inequities – is of concern to school choice critics. They argue that the ways in which school choice policies are implemented exacerbate inequality and commonly segregate and advantage the middle class; this provides further positional advantages for these parents, who can negotiate alternative school provisions to their advantage: "The exercise of choice as a process of maintaining social distinctions and educational differentiations, as related to social class and the class composition of schools, is likely to exaggerate social segregation" (Gewirtz et al., 1995, p. 91).

Parents as Active Choosers: Habitus, Agency, and Forms of Rationality

Most school choice plans are based on the assumption that all parents will engage in school selection in a similarly goal-oriented and self-interested fashion. The belief is that parents are "utility maximizers," who make decisions from clear value preferences based on rational calculations of costs, benefits, and probabilities of success; are able to demand action from local schools and teachers; and can be relied on to pursue the best interests of their children (Bosetti, 2004; Hatcher, 1998; Wells, 1997). However, the context of parental decision making is far more complex than just individual, rational decision making. It is part of a social process influenced by salient properties of social class and networks of social relationships (Bauch & Goldring, 1995; Bosetti, 2000; Coleman, 1988; Reay & Ball, 2005) and needs to take into account the role of human agency, the freedom and ability of parents to act independently, and the social and cultural practices that influence or guide their decision making (Bosetti, 2004; Goldthorpe & Jackson, 2008; Wells, 1997).

Cultural theorists help to explain the complexity of how social values limit or expand the horizon of what individuals determine to be reasonable goals of what they can achieve. These theorists argue that children are not socialized into the values of society as a whole; rather, they are socialized into a culture that corresponds with their class. Bourdieu (1986) argued that cultural expectations, values, and beliefs constitute a predisposition or "habitus," which equips a person for life in society. Habitus can be defined as "the acquired, socially constituted dispositions of social agents, to the classificatory principles they use, and the organizing principles of the action that they undertake without conscious planning" (Bourdieu, 1986, p. 241). The notion of habitus highlights the ways in which individuals internalize (or become enculturated) into particular social practices with little critical reflection. As the subjective incorporation or internalization of social structure, habitus has the effect of making the social world seem natural and its practices as taken for granted (Lingard & Christie, 2003). Life chances for both material and social status are determined by the individual's relationship to the volume of capital – economic or financial, human (knowledge, skills), social, and cultural – understood as a set of actually usable resources and powers (Wright, 2008). People's habitus, or culturally conditioned disposition, forms their rationality about how they consider potential risks and gains, and other factors that influence decisions, regarding which options are more viable than others. Wright has argued that decisions can be understood as a form of "practical sense" that operates intuitively and without effort. Deeply held values and beliefs constitute individuals' cultural inheritance, which informs the mental models or unconscious cultural processes that reflect their social origins.

The notion of habitus is significant when we consider parents' ability to negotiate the various alternative education programs in diversified school districts. For middle-class families, choosing a school is typically a family process, where children and parents are involved in mapping out alternative courses of action and choosing among them (Lareau & Weininger, 2008). Teachers, tutors, and counsellors are commonly consulted, as are other sources in parents' social networks. Parents' informal knowledge of the education system and conception of the significance of postsecondary education is central to students' success in navigating the application process.

A. Taylor and Woollard's (2003) Canadian study of parental selection of high schools in Alberta supported these findings. Participants' comments reflected different perspectives on parents' responsibility in selecting schools and the anxiety involved in making this decision. A middle-class parent acknowledged this burden and frustration in choosing a school:

> You feel that pressure for them [children] to succeed. If I hear "compete in the global economy" one more time I think I will scream ... But you do feel yourself getting sucked into it. I experienced the same feelings when my brother's kids took every instrument on the planet, Japanese and German and dancing ... And I'm thinking, "Oh my God; my kids are going to be left behind." But I think that's nuts and I told [my son], "If you don't do as well in high school as you're hoping to do or you think you should do and you decide you want to go and be a phys ed teacher, for example, you can go back to high school for another year." I just think what we do to these kids is inhuman. (A. Taylor & Woollard, 2003, p. 626)

In this case, despite the parent's frustration over perceived pressure to enrol children in activities that go beyond what children should be reasonably expected to do, the parent feels that she must conform to these expectations for her children not to be disadvantaged in their future prospects. This parent has internalized the established educational social structures, and while she criticizes them, she has nonetheless taken for granted that this is the path that she too must follow.

Empirical evidence from economists and psychologists highlights similar findings. The way in which choice theories are often conceptualized may underemphasize the way in which individuals actually make decisions. Choices are bound by the context in which they occur and limited by how rational an individual is when making a decision. Factors regarding the level of "risk and potential gain and marginal channel factors that make some options more accessible than others, all have a decisive impact on the decision that is made" (Ben-Porath, 2009, p. 532). Ben-Porath (2009) has noted the "bounded rationality" of parents, such as their reluctance to move their children out of failing schools. Referring to recent studies in the United States, Ben-Porath reported "the vast majority (up to 97%) of parents with children in 'failing' schools choose to keep their children in those schools, even when it is their legal right to do otherwise" (2009, p. 534).

In contrast to middle-class parents, working-class parents tend to be less involved in the decision-making process, reflecting an orientation to "accomplishment of natural growth" (Lareau, 2002, p. 748). Specifically, this stance suggests that children need to be cared for and protected, but they will develop and thrive spontaneously (Lareau & Weininger, 2008). A working-class parent reflected this sentiment in the following comment:

> When I just had one kid, I thought raising them was 80 percent nurturing and 20 percent nature, and I now think it's 20 percent nurturing and 80 percent nature. So I think it depends mainly on the kid – their personality, needs, etc. You can have the most perfect school, and if a kid is going to try something or look for … trouble, I don't know how much you can control that. (A. Taylor & Woollard, 2003, p. 625)

Working-class parents are less likely to challenge school authority and view "the school" (teachers and counsellors) to be responsible for providing the necessary guidance and support for students to select pathways to higher education or work. In this sense, parents are not active social agents in informing the way their child is educated; they rely on educational structures to direct their child. While this is an acceptable position to take, those children may not have the same level of access to alternative provisions of education as other children. The assumption is that when given the opportunity, parents will assess a variety of school choice programs and shop around to find the one that best fits the needs of the child. Yet clearly this is not the case in many instances.

This is not to suggest that parents are irrational in their decision making; rather, their values and habitus filter what factors, priorities, or utilities they seek to maximize in their choice of schools. For example, Goldthorpe and Jackson (2008) have argued that for families from less advantaged backgrounds, school achievement can be a crucial factor in their children's chances for upward mobility; however, pursuing more ambitious educational options typically entails risk in terms of costs and benefits. For families from more advantaged backgrounds, school achievement is not as critical because their children have other resources available to them to ensure they maintain their parents' social positioning (Goldthorpe & Jackson, 2008, p. 109).

Negotiating the system to make advantageous school choice decisions highlights the potential inequalities between active and inactive choosers.

This difference is displayed in another parent's difficulty in knowing how to make informed decisions regarding which school would best suit the needs of his child:

> What I really struggle with in parenting, and this was the perfect exercise, is we weren't taught to make choices; we were told what to do. So to have a process that I have to go through to make a decision and make it fair and legitimate is a huge test of my ability. So what I struggled with, the stress I had, was am I making this a fair and responsible decision? ... I didn't know what kind of spreadsheet was going to give us the right decision. It's like you're looking for the right equation and that was a pressure for me. I didn't know how to do it. (A. Taylor & Woollard, 2003, p. 623)

Assuming parents will make informed judgments about their child's education also assumes they are able to rationally synthesize and analyse the range of programs offered in the school district and assess these program offerings in relation to their child's learning needs and preferences. In effect, it relies on parents to choose well among a variety of educational options. Very quickly, the task of choosing becomes a complex endeavour. How parents negotiate this choice is entwined in how they access and manage relevant information within the constraints of their own limited time and resources, what they deem to be quality education, and what sort of educational experience they desire for their child.

Middle-Class Anxiety, School Choice, and Intensive Forms of Parenting

Since the late 1970s, a discernible shift has occurred from an industrial, resourced-based economy to a globally interconnected, knowledge-based economy in which intellectual capabilities are as critical as other economic resources (Drucker, 1993; Friesen, Clifford, Jacobsen, & Jardine, 2005; Friesen, Clifford, & Lock, 2004). The rules and practices that determined success in the industrial economy have changed, with more social pressure to accumulate academic qualifications as a reflection of intellectual capital, thereby increasing competition for access to higher education. This focus has created what Collins (1979) described as a *credential society*, in which eligibility for work is determined by certificates or degrees that may or may not be relevant to the job.

Transition to a credential society in a knowledge economy has increased anxiety among middle-class parents regarding their ability to maintain their socio-economic status and secure educational advantage for their children. Career advancement through the labour market has become increasingly risky as evidenced by unstable global markets and significant disruption in middle-class careers (Power et al., 2003). As a result, middle-class parents have become more prudent in selecting schools (Avis, 2003; Bourdieu & Boltanski, 1978; P. Brown, 2000; T. Hill & Guin, 2003). They are most likely to "seek 'the right kind of education' for their children so as to secure a competitive edge in what they regard as the 'main site of social selection'" (Power et al., 2003, p. 2). For these parents, education is a positional good. Motivated by fear of downward mobility, parents believe that the educational success of their children is too important to be left to the chance outcome of an open competition and instead seek competitive advantage through independent or specialized schools (P. Brown, 1997, p. 402).

When parents choose schools, they are not seeking merely "quality" education, but are also expressing the values they are attempting to foster in their children (Power, 2004, p. 25). When such goals are not met in a particular educational environment, parents feel anxious that their children may not flourish. For example, the following comment from a parent selecting an elementary school illustrates the importance of values in her choice: "Beth: It is about values, NOT test scores. We want a school environment where Christian values go right through the culture of the whole school and don't get watered down" (Bosetti & Pyryt, 2007, p. 101). Beth's point highlights her perception that mainstream schooling will not harmonize with her family's religious values. She seeks schooling where core Christian values are central to learning and integrated throughout the school community.

In a very different context, another parent, Kate, resists the homogeneity of her middle-class neighbourhood. She noted,

> I was looking for a school with an open-minded environment where differences are accepted. I wanted a school where my son could explore ideas, ask questions and be challenged. I didn't want him to attend some middle-class school in suburbia where everyone is the same. (Bosetti & Pyryt, 2007, p. 101)

A common concern expressed in the school choice debate is that with middle-class parents' heightened awareness and anxiety in securing future life chances (career opportunities) for their children, they are both hypersensitive and overly vigilant in considering the options that will best maximize their children's success.

Brittany: I want to be sure that [our daughter] maintains her 91% average in high school. We are looking into sending her to the Renaissance School in Italy [for grade 12]. There are only 4 to 6 kids in a class, and our friend's daughter went and she was admitted to all the universities she applied to. (Bosetti & Pyryt, 2007, p. 103)

The majority of alternative education programs offered in the two largest public school districts in Alberta (Edmonton Public School Board and Calgary Board of Education) appear to target educational mandates that cater to and ease middle-class angst. In educational markets where schools compete for students and are ranked by student achievement on standardized tests, savvy schools offer alternative programs with specializations that focus on high performance athletes, gifted education, science and technology, or foreign languages. This not only gives students an extra advantage in their later years but also attracts high achieving, academically able students. Although a clear range of alternative programs are offered in these school districts (Aboriginal education, trades and technology, alternative program for at-risk youth), the vast majority are targeted to advancing student achievement through specialized learning (International Baccalaureate programs, science schools, single-gender schools).

For students in minority or low-income groups, these sorts of specialized programs are not viable options. They quickly come to understand that they do not share the same "language" (as defined by culture, tradition, values, and beliefs) as the dominant class of students, nor do they resonate with the curriculum being offered. They find their educational experience of little relevance and vote with their feet by leaving the education system as early as possible or choosing a less ambitious route. They come to understand that their chances of success in educational attainment are small, and in realistically assessing the possible futures available to them, they choose their neighbourhood school. If that does not meet their needs, they pursue paid work rather than an education that does not reflect their interests or needs (Bowles & Jensen, 2001).

Lucey and Reay (2002) examined how children from professional, middle-class families in the United Kingdom were pushed towards high performance as a response to their parents' anxiety about getting them into the "right school." They suggested that parents who failed to get their child into a selective school, and who were not in a financial position to buy a home in the catchment area of a high-performing school or send their child to a private school, were more likely to push for their child to be placed in an accelerated or enriched program (Lucey & Reay, 2002, p. 333). They found that accelerated and enhanced programs tended to tap into middle-class feelings around cleverness, potential, and entitlement. They uncovered an implicit assumption in the narratives of middle-class parents and teachers that these children are

> "bright," "clever" and, above all, "have potential." The great unspoken is that the superior educational performance of the middle classes is a demonstration of an innate higher intelligence and the lower performance of the working classes of their relative intellectual dullness. Middle-class children may be much more likely to be viewed as displaying all those qualities which naturally point towards "talent" and "giftedness." (Lucey & Reay, 2002, p. 333)

The labelling of children as *clever, bright,* or *having potential* plays into the positional advantage of middle-class families who may be better able to negotiate a particular school for their child.

The Gifted and Talented Education program (GATE) in the Calgary Board of Education is an example of a program that serves a limited number of academically gifted students. The Calgary Board of Education currently serves gifted learners (IQ 130, plus or minus 5; WISC-IV; Canadian norms) in congregated settings (special programs for selected students in grades 4 to 12) or by provision through an individualized program plan where the child is accommodated in his or her designated community school. A GATE admissions committee determines which students should be accepted into the program and which students should remain in their community school. At the elementary level, teachers identify potentially gifted students and recommend them for assessment by school board psychologists. Parents unwilling to leave a referral to chance have their child assessed independently by a psychologist in private practice at a typical cost of $1000. Some parents shop around for a psychologist who will run a battery of tests and write a report that highlights their child's strengths. Some push to have their child double coded (e.g., gifted and learning disabled) to compensate for a borderline score and create a better case for special placement in the GATE program (Bosetti & Pyryt, 2007).

The following quote reflects a parent's commitment to have his child admitted to the GATE program:

> Peter: We knew our son was gifted but for some reason the board didn't want to have him tested. They were willing to provide enrichment activities for him, but [our son] just saw that as piling on more work. We had him tested

and moved him into the public system where they have the GATE program. If he didn't get into GATE, then our second option was to try to get him into [Name] charter school [for gifted students]. (Bosetti & Pyryt, 2007, p. 102)

Parents with the requisite social networks and economic resources can find options that compensate for the initial disappointment of not qualifying for the GATE program and still ensure advantage for their children.

Morgan: We had all three of our girls tested. Hilary didn't quite qualify for GATE. She was so disappointed, but we learned where she had to work to improve her grades. We now know what to expect from our girls. Mia goes to [tutorial service] on Saturdays to work on her math, and Senna went to the Reading Foundation to improve her reading. (Bosetti & Pyryt, 2007, p. 102)

Parents have a legitimate right to use their resources to find schools that meet their children's needs; however, equality of opportunity and the efficacy of alternative programs targeted to meet special needs are compromised when parents circumvent the process by "playing the system" and hiring a sympathetic psychologist or providing extra tutorial services. This undermines the basic premise that qualified children will be treated equally when they are considered for a specialized program, and it unfairly advantages middle-class parents with the ability to access and pay for independent assessments. Yet such parental attempts to secure better credentials for their children are common.

Some school districts have attempted to close the equity gap by allocating alternative programs to neighbourhood schools with declining enrolment or poor academic success rates. For example, in Alberta, alternative choice programs have commonly been introduced in undersubscribed inner-city public schools, therein removing economic barriers for families who would not otherwise have the opportunity to send their children to these programs. The benefits are twofold. First, alternative programs attract more students (and families) to an undersubscribed school threatened with closure (D. Ball, 2007). Second, they draw middle-class families who may have a vested interest in ensuring the educational program's success. Unfortunately, alternative programs can compromise the community-based program (D. Ball, 2007). Instead of empowering and providing more opportunities to inner-city children and their families, they are further disempowered and pushed aside by those attending from outside the catchment area.

D. Ball (2007) studied such a school, in which neighbourhood students were given the option of remaining in the regular school stream (which was designated to be phased out in three years); enrol in one of the two alternative programs, which were Mandarin-language immersion and a science-based program; or be bussed to their new designated school. The community shared the view that both the Mandarin-based and the science-based programs would provide academic enrichment and higher status than the undersubscribed neighbourhood school.

Of the 258 students from the community, 7 enrolled in the Mandarin program, 75 enrolled in the science program, and the remainder elected either to stay in the community program until it closed or move to the new designated school. Subtle attempts at exclusion and social closure are evident in the following comments from parents and teachers:

> Parent: There was quite a furor when they said we're going to get rid of the regular program and roll everything into the science program because parents were quite upset that they chose to be here, expecting a certain level, and there was a worry that it [including students from the neighbourhood] was going to drag down the level quite dramatically. (D. Ball, 2007, p. 171)
>
> Parent: I thought the student profile would act like a filter. It seems like students meeting the program's criteria would achieve entrance; but then I heard students from the neighbourhood had priority, whether they matched the profile or not. It doesn't seem right. (D. Ball, 2007, p. 169)
>
> Teacher: It's tough because this is their neighbourhood school, and they should have a right to come here, but they don't pay their [school program] fees, they aren't interested in science, and they disrupt the learning of students whose parents either drove them for an hour to be here, or paid their bus fees. It's difficult to justify. (D. Ball, 2007, p. 169)

Students in the Mandarin program were predominately Chinese, either Canadian born or recent immigrants to Canada. While 35% of students in this program had their bussing and program fees subsidized, which requires parents to access documents from the school board website and filling them out, only 3% of students had unpaid fees – which meant that their parents either did not apply for or did not qualify for subsidy but in any case did not pay the fees. In comparison, 40% of the students from the community had unpaid program fees and another 20% were subsidized (D. Ball, 2007). Although the students in the Mandarin program were from lower-income families, their parents had the social networks and education levels to successfully navigate their way through the system to find a relatively racially homogenous school community that resonated with their cultural values and traditions. These parents also had the capacity to access the government subsidies to enable their children to attend this school.

Victoria School of the Arts (formerly Victoria Composite High School) in Edmonton provides an example of how the local school board prevented community-based students from being marginalized from attending this alternative school. Located in a mature, inner-city neighbourhood, this high school was undersubscribed before its establishment as an arts-based performance school. The school became a magnet for students from numerous areas of the city who shared a common interest in the arts, and families moved to the area because they wanted their children to attend the school (A. Taylor, 2001b). Administrators proposed selective admission requirements necessitating a portfolio. The Edmonton Public School Board struck down this proposal on the grounds that it was unfair to local students, who would not be automatically accepted for admission despite this being their designated school (Sands, 2013).

In Alberta, charter schools are another option within the publically funded education system. These schools provide opportunities for parents, educators, and other stakeholder groups to fulfil a particular mandate (charter) without the economic barriers inherent in independent schools. Charter schools receive the same funding as public schools and cannot charge tuition or have a religious affiliation. In some cases they specifically target marginalized groups who experience cultural, social, or economic barriers in accessing programs that effectively address the learning needs of their children (e.g., Boyle Street Education Centre, a program for at-risk youth; the Mother Earth's Children's Charter School, for Indigenous students; and Almadina Language Charter Academy, for students for whom English is a second language; Bosetti, 1998a, 2001).

On the one hand, charter schools' specified educational mandates provide a clear directive and curricular focus; on the other, doing so may limit the diversity of the student population. For instance, the Alberta Teachers' Association has taken a critical stance against charter schools, arguing they attract highly desirable, "easy to teach" students:

> Now charters compete for the most successful students in the poorest communities, or they accept all applicants and push the low performers back into the public school system ... It matters not that the original proponents of charter schools had different goals. It does matter, though, that charter schools have become in many communities a force intended to disrupt the

traditional notion of public schooling. (Ravitch, 2010, as quoted in Alberta Teachers' Association, 2011, p. 6)

While little large-scale research has been conducted to verify whether this disruption has been the case in Alberta, charter school sceptics have the perception that because these schools do not have the funding to provide the same level of learning support available in the larger public system, charter schools do not accept children who have specific learning challenges. In light of the limited range of support services available and the nature of the charter mandate, these schools may limit access to students with particular learning or behavioural difficulties. Whether intentional or not, charter schools are perceived to create a creaming effect by taking more desirable students. In so doing, the schools create niche educational mandates that privilege certain forms of knowledge for desirable demographic groups.

This limited access is problematic in at least two ways. First, developing alternative programs that privilege certain disciplines over others, such as classical education over vocational, may create a hierarchy wherein certain values and credentials are perceived to have greater worth than others. Second, students who do not conform to the particular educational mandate may choose not to attend such a school and may consequently feel of lesser worth than children who do conform. The perceived higher-valued credentials a child receives by attending a specialized program may come at a cost to students who do not have a similar educational distinction.

Hidden Costs of Programs of Choice

Securing a place in a school of choice involves both active and informed participation by parents to consider, evaluate, and apply for admission. At a basic level, this work involves the time and labour necessary for parents to consider the available options both within and beyond public education systems. Yet even when parents choose an alternative program in the public education system, they incur a number of expenses despite the intent of making programs of choice publically available and tuition free. Expenses that some parents may simply not be able to afford include transportation to and from school, uniforms, extracurricular activities or field trips, and supplemental tutoring (D. Ball, 2007).

One of the clear challenges in public school districts is the issue of school bus transportation costs. Sprawling urban areas with schools over capacity, burgeoning suburbs with affordable housing for families with young children, and the geographical challenges of serving sparsely populated rural areas make affordable transportation a pressing and common concern for superintendents across Canada. Larger public school districts attempt to minimize this extra cost by creating congregated bus schedules, whereby drop-off points are designated in residential areas. Another strategy has been to align non-instructional teaching days for all public and alternative schools so that transportation costs can be reduced on those days. Parents choosing a school or an alternative program outside the catchment area designated for their children may shoulder or supplement the base cost of transportation. If a public board is committed to choice and equity in access for students, then mechanisms to support additional costs of bussing must be considered.

Support for additional bussing costs has proven more challenging for charter schools and independent schools. Given the school's smaller budgets, charter school parents may incur higher transportation costs than parents whose children attend other public schools (Cuthberson, 2012, p. 4). In one district, the discrepancy between attending an alternative public school and attending a charter school is an additional $295 per year. Such discrepancies elucidate the financial barriers that may prevent families from enrolling their children in a charter school. Independent schools may simply place transportation costs fully on parents wanting to use the service, as an extra cost of attending the school. It is important to acknowledge that transportation fee differentials may not be an overt attempt by charter schools or alternative programs to limit the number of families with lower-socio-economic standing from enrolling. It nonetheless creates hidden mechanisms that dissuade poorer families from considering a charter school or independent school for their children.

While uniform-dress policies have been a long-standing tradition of independent schools, such policies are increasingly present in alternative and charter schools in Canada. Four reasons for implementing specific uniform policies are commonly cited in the literature (Gereluk, 2008). First, the use of school uniforms attempts to reduce social stratification among students: having everyone wear one set uniform removes obvious distinctions between poor and wealthy students, so less advantaged students will not be socially excluded based on their attire. Second, schools hope that uniform-dress policies will reduce discipline problems and generally improve student behaviour. This is based on the argument that the absence of labels, logos, or provocative clothing will be less distracting and lead to decreased tension among students. Third, uniforms are an outward manifestation of the school's values; most schools have some form of dress code to help instil pride and attachment to that particular school. Finally, some suggest a correlation exists between wearing uniforms and improved achievement. The claim is that improved behaviour and sense of pride and cohesion transfer to students' studies. By not focusing on what others are wearing, students instead focus on the central task of learning.

It is unclear whether the reasons noted above have merit, but educators and families nonetheless hold the perception that uniforms provide students with a positive correlation to the ethos of the school. As a result, schools may adopt and present a school uniform policy as a perceived added benefit. If parents send their child to the school, they must pay for the uniforms. For middle-class parents who want to provide their child with a slight advantage and enjoy the status associated with attending a specialist school, this additional cost may be seen as a necessary burden. For lower-income families, however, it creates another financial obstacle.

While transportation and school uniform costs are generally explicit on school and district websites, other costs, such as extracurricular activities, field trips, and tutoring, may be hidden. A common hidden cost is incurred when parents agree to support their child's development in a particular skill by providing supplementary activities. This cost is common in elite performing arts or athletics schools. The expectation is that for the child to do well in the school environment, parents must commit to the extra costs incurred by attending competitions, workshops, or training seminars. Implicit in these expectations is that parents will supplement curricular activities with additional lessons or tutoring outside school hours in support of that skill or talent. Attending a hockey school, for instance, will inevitably mean extra practices, tournaments, and equipment for the child. The goal in such a school is not mere participation in hockey but excellence in that endeavour. Both the explicitly stated costs (such as transportation fees, field trips, or uniforms) and the implicit expectations (such as supplemental lessons, tutoring, or activities beyond school hours) necessarily limit the socio-economic groups that can take advantage of this alternative provision of schooling.

Conclusion

School choice has an important role in Canadian society in terms of accommodating increased diversity; preserving and enhancing minority culture, language, and identity; and engaging learners by addressing their learning needs, preferences, and family values. Government regulations can mitigate some of the inequities created by schools of choice, including alternative, charter, and independent schools, by developing funding provisions to allow children of economically disadvantaged families and those with special needs to attend schools of choice. Governments can provide mechanisms for instructional grants to follow children to their school of choice through tax credits, vouchers, or weighted funding formulas. Governments can likewise ensure quality by regulating choice and accreditation of alternative and independent schools. However, despite well-designed policies, the sociocultural and psychological factors that influence how and why parents engage in school choice, along with current intensive parenting practices, affect the impact of school choice policies and public education in various contexts.

It seems unreasonable to hold parents, who advocate on behalf of their children by selecting schools of choice, responsible for the education system's failure to address issues of equity and diversity. School districts choose whether to extend themselves on behalf of parents who lack the resources or the sociocultural capital to intervene effectively for their children (Fried, 1998). Clearly, school choice and an unfettered educational marketplace are no substitute for state intervention and government policy that ensures the social, emotional, and learning needs of all children.

The following is a summary of key themes covered in this chapter with implications for policy:

1 Competitive educational markets created by school choice policies can obscure the aims of public education as a vehicle for children to, through their natural abilities and effort, develop their potential, achieve credentials, and transcend their social location. When jurisdictions develop school choice policies that respond primarily to pressures created by a competitive educational market, meeting parental demand and competing for student enrolment rather than providing programs based on pedagogical innovation or student learning needs, they may inadvertently be contributing to the creation of a two-tiered education system. That is to say, they have not created sufficient policies and processes to ensure equity in access.

2 School choice programs necessitate marketing to and recruiting students, with the aim of attracting students who would benefit from the mandate of the specialist program (elite athlete, gifted learner, at-risk youth). It is difficult for policymakers to alleviate parental anxiety

inherent in the process of choosing the right school, ensuring their child is admitted to the desired program, and selecting a program appropriate for the learning needs of the child. While schools may create admission policies to facilitate admitting students who would benefit from the school, based on natural ability and effort, savvy parents have learned how to navigate the system and provide advantages for their children.

3   In a competitive system, some school districts are compelled to respond to market demand and provide schools that accommodate lifestyle choices and niche markets. Examples are schools devoted to athletes and performing artists (musicians, dancers) and those with particular curricular focus (art, science, language immersion) or philosophical orientation (single gender, Waldorf, Montessori). While these programs address parental desires and the educational needs of students, they do not respond to issues of equality of opportunity, address the needs of marginalized groups, or target the improved academic performance of low-achieving students from economically disadvantaged families. School boards have attempted to mitigate inequity by locating programs of choice within existing neighbourhood schools in low-income areas; however, it is difficult for policymakers to address the culture of choice, social closure, and social and cultural capital that comes with middle-class advantage.

4   The reality is that class advantages exist and are exacerbated by apprehension of an unstable world economy and the future of work. Media focus on the competitive ranking of schools and school systems at the international, national, and regional level contributes to anxiety regarding the quality of public education and the level of public confidence that schools are adequately preparing students for the twenty-first century and work in a global market. This anxiety fuels parents' desire to secure positional advantage for their children in trying to attain desirable educational credentials in a knowledge-based economy.

6

Ethical Principles to Guide School Choice Policies in Canada

In the preceding chapters, we explored the philosophical basis for school choice policies, the evolution of school choice policies across Canada, and the ways in which parents make choices for their children's education. In the United States, school choice policies have centred on failing schools, market competition, racial integration, and the needs of poor and racial minority groups. In contrast, school choice policies in Canada have been more focused on providing educational opportunities that respond to the diversity in Canadian culture, including provisions for alternative programs that provide a sense of belonging and identity for national and immigrant minority groups, as well as disenfranchised youth. While Canada has a long history of adopting school choice policies to accommodate language, religion, and culture, it has only been since the late 1980s that school choice policies have been adopted as an instrument for education reform. Since that time, a growing movement in Canada has called for more schooling options to foster innovation and greater program variation to accommodate parents' voice and choice in the way their children are educated.

While not every jurisdiction embraces it enthusiastically, most policymakers across Canada currently accept the idea that parents should have options regarding the location of their child's school and the types of accessible programs. But even given this general agreement, opinions vary regarding the kinds of school choice policies that should be introduced and how they should be implemented. To address these debates in this final chapter, we offer a series of specific recommendations to guide policymakers and help concerned citizens to navigate the issues that provisions for school choice present.

We argue that policy recommendations must be guided by overarching ethical and moral principles that offer a coherent justification as to why particular school choice policies should be introduced. Noting that provisions for school choice have sometimes been introduced in an ad hoc manner, or denied on ideological grounds, we additionally engage the empirical research to help us determine which school choice options have been shown to realize particular educational aims. However, in offering specific recommendations related to demands by parents and communities for greater choice in how their children are educated, it is not our intention to defend particular policies unconditionally. Many of the educational issues we explore in this chapter, including funding and autonomy for First Nations schooling and faith-based schools, are highly controversial and are often worked out within an emotionally charged public context. By offering specific policy recommendations, our ultimate aim is to highlight the need for more considered deliberation regarding the role and purpose of schooling within a democratic society.

We have divided this chapter into three parts. In the first section, we explore how liberal multiculturalism (Kymlicka, 1998, 2007) can offer important insights into accommodating ethnocultural diversity. Offering specific policy recommendations based on this philosophical framework, we argue that school choice policies must involve group-differentiated approaches that attend to the unique aspirations and needs of particular minority communities and students from them. As we have explored in previous chapters, for historical and constitutional reasons, the kinds of school policies appropriate for Aboriginal students and communities differ considerably from policies seeking to serve ethnic minority populations originally from, for example, Ukraine or Pakistan. Although the school choice policies we outline for ethnic minority groups offer fairer terms for integration into the mainstream society, education accommodations for national minority groups involve elements of self-government and autonomy to enable them to sustain themselves as distinct and unique cultures.

In the second section, seeking ethical and moral principles to guide school choice policies without limiting educational accommodations exclusively to the liberal multicultural focus on ethnocultural diversity, we examine how Rawls's liberal theory (1993, 1999) offers a philosophical rationale for a robust range of school choice policies that meet the diverse needs of students in a way that can maintain and promote a more egalitarian society. In contrast to the principles of liberal multiculturalism, school choice policies informed by liberal theory prioritize considerations concerning the specific, individual interests of the child, and in particular those most disadvantaged in society. Drawing on the values of ethical individualism, we argue that evaluating and offering recommendations around school choice policies must consider the overarching principles of autonomy, liberty, and opportunity. However, in adopting liberal theory as a guide in making policy recommendations, we believe these principles must be weighed in relation to Rawls's (1999) difference principle, which asserts that particular school choice policies should be introduced only if they are to the benefit of the least advantaged members of society. Coupling the notion of ethical individualism with the difference principle ensures that particular accommodations for children will not create further disadvantages to already marginalized student populations.

In the final section, we consider the extent to which neoliberal principles emphasizing increased competition through the marketization of schools should guide school choice policy decisions. After explaining how neoliberal policies seek to create greater choice in schooling options through various mechanisms of competition among schools, using empirical research and arguments developed in the first two sections of this chapter, we point out the limitations of using a neoliberal framework to guide provisions for school choice. Specifically, we argue that this philosophical framework's overreliance on free market ideology is bereft of the ethical and moral principles needed to make sound policy decisions that serve groups beyond the most privileged in society.

Liberal Multiculturalism and School Choice Policies

Two of the primary aims of school choice policies are to accommodate and support ethnocultural diversity. As we have seen in previous chapters, Canada has historically responded to diversity – at least for francophones and Roman Catholics. Today, provisions for autonomous and fully funded francophone and Catholic school districts are relatively uncontroversial. However, this is not the case regarding how schools in Aboriginal communities should be funded and administered or whether provincial jurisdictions should provide partial or full funding for heritage-language programs, faith-based schools, or Africentric schools. These sorts of schooling options have become the focus of highly contentious public debates. Residing at the heart of these debates are fears of ethnic separatism and concerns as to the extent to which public money should be allocated to preserve and promote the distinct ethnocultural and linguistic identities of particular minority groups. We argue that liberal multiculturalism (Kymlicka, 1998, 2007) provides a comprehensive philosophical framework for how policymakers can best address the majority of these debates.

According to Kymlicka (2007), to understand the nature of liberal multiculturalism, it is helpful to appreciate what it is a response to and a reaction against (p. 61). Following Kymlicka's (2007) line of reasoning, all struggles for multiculturalism share a rejection of the unitary and homogenous nation-state ideal, where a single dominant national group uses its power to privilege and promote its own language, culture, history, and religion. Within the unitary nation-state model, non-dominant ethnocultural groups are subject to an array of nation-building policies meant to assimilate them and, as was the case for Aboriginal peoples in Canada, eradicate their unique cultural and linguistic identities. Nation-building policies include the creation of a national system of education accompanied by a standardized curriculum that all children must learn and all schools must follow. To advance the aims of creating a homogenous nation-state, within this state-imposed common curriculum, the dominant group's language, culture, and history are promoted and normalized as the *national* language, culture, and history (Gereluk & Scott, 2014). As we explored in Chapters 2 and 3, this model of citizenship occurred in Canada, wherein descendants of settlers from the British Isles used schooling as a means to impose the English language, as well as Anglo values and cultural traditions, on the larger population.

In rejecting this unitary nation-state model, Kymlicka (2007) argued that liberal multiculturalism begins with repudiating the idea that the state belongs to the dominant national group; it belongs equally to all citizens regardless of their ethnic, racial, or cultural background. In upholding this principle, the state has a responsibility to replace "assimilationist and exclusionary nation-building policies with policies of recognition and accommodation" (Kymlicka, 2007, p. 66). Educational policies inspired by liberal multiculturalism can include providing Aboriginal communities with greater autonomy and control over education, revising the history curricula in schools to give greater attention to the participation and contribution of formally marginalized ethnocultural groups, and introducing bilingual language programs for children of immigrants.

These differences do not mean, however, that Canada's liberal multicultural policies have abandoned nation building entirely. Almost all schools in Canada continue to require students to learn at least one of the two official languages and observe national holidays like Remembrance Day. Such attempts at promoting greater cohesion and unity reflect a belief that a democratic society cannot survive unless a diverse citizenry has the linguistic means to communicate with one another, holds a set of core liberal democratic values in common, and possesses a measure of respect towards the country's political institutions. Thus, rather than replacing nation-building policies, multicultural policies supplement and transform them so they are less likely to marginalize minority groups. As Kymlicka (2007) outlined, "The resulting approach is best described as one in which robust forms of nation building are combined and constrained by robust forms of minority rights" (p. 83).

In conferring specific rights for minority groups, Kymlicka (2007) further asserted the theory and principles of liberal multiculturalism are highly group differentiated in that they make a clear distinction between rights for ethnic or immigrant minority groups and national minority peoples (pp. 66–77). Kymlicka (1998) defined national minority groups as "historically settled, territorially concentrated, and previously self-governing cultures whose territories have been incorporated into the larger state" (p. 30). As we examined in detail throughout Chapter 2, examples of national minority groups in Canada include Aboriginal peoples (i.e., First Nations peoples, Inuit, and Metis) and the Quebecois (Canada's French-speaking population). While the relationship of the Quebecois and particular Aboriginal national communities, like the Blackfoot and the Mi'kmaq, to the Canadian state are fundamentally different, they share a strong link as founding partners in the Canadian federation. Therefore, they have a right to forms of territorial autonomy, self-government, and language rights. By negotiating new political arrangements, multicultural policies targeting national minority groups seek to preserve elements of their pre-existing institutional separateness so they can sustain themselves as distinct linguistic and cultural communities.

Alongside national minority groups, Kymlicka (1998) defined ethnic minority groups as people who have chosen to leave their country to start life in a new country. By making the decision to emigrate, immigrant groups have generally understood that they are entering a country with already established laws and institutions (Kymlicka, 1998, p. 7). Accordingly, ethnic minority groups, including groups who have lived in Canada for many generations, as is the case with Canadians of Chinese and Ukrainian descent, have normally not sought institutional separation and autonomy similar to national minority groups. Rather, ethnic minority groups have pursued fairer terms for integration into their adopted country. As a result, under a liberal multicultural framework, policies targeting ethnic minority groups aim to reduce barriers and stigmas that limit their ability to fully participate in mainstream society and government institutions.

With the distinction between these two minority groups in mind, liberal multiculturalism should therefore not be seen as "a single unified struggle in the name of 'diversity'" (Kymlicka, 2007, p. 79). Rather, it should be understood as "the outcome of multiple struggles by different types of ethno-cultural groups, mobilizing along different legal and administrative tracks" (Kymlicka, 2007, p. 79). Although it is not in the scope of this chapter to highlight all the various strategies drawn from a liberal multicultural framework that could respond to the unique challenges and aspirations of national and ethnic minority peoples, we want to focus on a number of prominent educational issues that policymakers across Canada contend with today.

Francophones

The principles of liberal multiculturalism in relation to national minority groups can be seen in historic accommodations to the Quebecois within the British North America Act of 1867. By devolving authority over education and language to the provincial level, in Quebec, where the Quebecois formed a demographic majority, the Quebecois gained control of the mechanisms needed to guarantee their ongoing continuation as a French-speaking society within the Canadian federation. As part of this multinational political framework, the government of Quebec has been able to enact nation-building policies of its own, paralleling those enacted by anglophones in the rest of Canada. This control has included passing laws making it mandatory for all non-anglophone immigrants entering Quebec to send their children to schools within the mainstream francophone system, thus ensuring that French remains the dominant language.

Other educational policies related to francophones in Canada that reflect the principles of liberal multiculturalism include parental rights to send their children to publically funded primary and secondary schools where instruction occurs exclusively in French, as long as numbers warrant and regardless of where they live in Canada. Under a multicultural policy framework, these francophone schools, which exist within a separate school district, receive the same (or higher) funding as anglophone schools and are managed and governed by francophones. Today, francophones have secured these accommodations within Section 23 of the Canadian Charter of Rights and Freedoms (Government of Canada,

2014a), which, building on provisions in the British North America Act, provides constitutional guarantees for minority French-language education in all provinces and territories outside Quebec. These same constitutional provisions have additionally guaranteed full funding for Catholic school boards in Ontario, Alberta, and Saskatchewan.[1]

Because of rights guaranteed in the Charter of Rights and Freedoms, francophone parents have been able to successfully pursue legal action to ensure schools for their children provide the same level of facilities and funding as non-francophone schools. For example, after a five-year legal battle, in April of 2015 parents of children attending the francophone school École-Rose-des-Vents in Vancouver won a Supreme Court of Canada case arguing that conditions in their school, including its overall size and access to library resources, lagged far behind nearby English-language schools ("Vancouver Francophone Parents," 2015). While the decision in favour of these parents' claims garnered some public attention, the right of Franco-Canadians to access equally funded, institutionally separate French-language schools is a largely uncontroversial part of the school choice landscape in Canada.

Aboriginal peoples

Today, Aboriginal communities in Canada are lobbying the federal government to secure the same rights and level of institutional autonomy that francophone communities possess. According to one study, band-run schools operate on budgets that are 25% lower than provincially run schools (Bell et al., 2004). In addition, academic achievement in these schools lags far behind that of non-Aboriginal students. For instance, the Assembly of First Nations (2012) found that only 39% of First Nations people 20 to 24 years of age had completed high school, whereas 87% of other Canadians in that demographic had graduated. In the spring of 2014, the federal government, under increasing pressure to address these concerns, introduced Bill C-33: The First Nations Control of First Nations Education Act (Parliament of Canada, 2014). This bill would have provided an estimated $1.9 billion in new funding to on-reserve schools.

---

1 This was the case for Newfoundland as well until 1995, when the government replaced the denominational school system with a single secular system.

However, to receive this money, band-run schools had to ensure they offered an education program where students would be able "to obtain a recognized high school diploma and to move between education systems without impediment" (Parliament of Canada, 2014, para. 7). Although National Chief of the Assembly of First Nations Shawn Atleo supported the bill, it was met with immediate opposition from many leaders in the Aboriginal community. Social activist and Indigenous law professor Palmater (2014), for instance, argued that Bill C-33 had been introduced without proper consultation with Aboriginal communities. Moreover, it "increased ministerial control over education in very paternalistic ways (including co-managers and third-party managers of education); it did not guarantee specific levels of funding; and English and French were made the languages of instruction" (Palmater, 2014, p. 1). In place of this agreement, a number of First Nations leaders demanded the government put jurisdiction over education in the hands of Aboriginal communities so these schools could offer educational environments more responsive to the cultural and linguistic traditions of their communities (Assembly of First Nations, 2012). Because of sustained criticism like this, Atleo elected to step down as national chief rather than continue championing the bill (Kennedy, 2014).

The constitutional guarantees that francophones in Canada have been able to secure to preserve and promote their unique cultural and linguistic identity offer a valuable template to guide policy considerations related to the controversies that surrounded the introduction of Bill C-33. Although it is not within the scope of this chapter to offer comprehensive policy proposals concerning First Nations education, by employing insights from a liberal multicultural framework we can sketch out some broad policy recommendations related to issues of school choice for Aboriginal parents and students. The first of these recommendations concerns funding levels, which are a matter of ongoing debate. Currently, some analysts argue that First Nations students attending on-reserve schools receive the same levels of funding as students in the provincially run system (Bains, 2014), rather than the oft-cited statistic of 25% less funding (Bell et al., 2004). Aboriginal Affairs and Northern Development (now called Indigenous and Northern Affairs Canada), which controls funding for on-reserve schools, concurs with this former view. However, Mendelson (2008) contradicts this claim:

The harsh reality is that the Department's confidence in the parity of its funding is misplaced, since it simply does not know. There are no regular data collected to compare provincial and federal education funding levels, nor is there any mechanism in the budget-setting process for First Nations education to ensure that funding levels are indeed comparable to those in provinces. (pp. 6–7)

Under the principles of liberal multiculturalism, this current state of affairs is unacceptable. Funding for First Nations students attending on-reserve schools must be at least equal to, if not more than, the per-student funding for non-Aboriginal students. While francophone parents have been able to successfully pursue legal action against provincial and territorial governments for failing to provide the same level of facilities and funding for francophone schools as that of English schools ("Vancouver Francophone Parents," 2015), because of an absence of any agreed-on mechanism to determine funding levels, Aboriginal parents and communities have not been able to seek similar forms of legal redress against the federal government. Although Bill C-33 sought to address funding levels, it did not include any clearly defined, legally binding mechanism to determine what these funding levels should be. As a result, the need is pressing to ensure funding levels and facilities in First Nations schools equal to those of other provincial schools.

In addition to parity in funding levels, a liberal multicultural framework would also uphold the principle that First Nations peoples and communities should have jurisdiction over education. While the federal government has constitutional and treaty obligations for on-reserve education, First Nations communities and leaders, paralleling rights for francophones, must have administrative control over education for their children. After more than a century of government attempts at assimilation, the need is urgent to move beyond colonial relationships in which the federal government decides what is best for Aboriginal peoples. This change does not mean that partnerships between First Nations and other organizations and levels of government cannot be forged. However, specific national communities require the ability to enter into particular agreements on their own terms and in ways that respond to their specific needs and aspirations.

Influenced by the theory and practice of liberal multiculturalism, one of the most striking examples includes the formation of Nunavut in 1999. Similar to circumstances in Quebec, Nunavut was created so that the Inuit would form a majority within their historic homeland, and thus maintain a level of institutional separateness that would give them greater ability to preserve and protect their distinct language and culture. As discussed in Chapter 2, through gaining political autonomy and language rights, Inuit leaders in Nunavut have been able to introduce – although not without challenges ("Nunavut Struggles," 2011) – a new education act focusing on ensuring that students receive partial instruction in their traditional language.

While other Aboriginal communities may not have the numbers to form a political territory, some have negotiated new agreements with federal and provincial or territorial governments that have increased educational funding levels and autonomy. For example, in 1999, Mi'kmaq communities created their own school board in Nova Scotia, securing the right to manage the education of their children for the first time in over a century (Canadian Education Association, 2015). According to a recent report, by 2011 the graduation rate for Mi'kmaq students in this school board had increased to 75%, and by 2013, 87% of students had graduated from high school (Mi'kmaw Kina'matnewey, 2014).

As these examples show, by using the principles of liberal multiculturalism to guide school choice policies for Aboriginal parents and communities, opportunities exist to increase levels of funding and better ensure that the traditional languages and cultures of specific First Nations communities are transmitted to the next generation of children and youth. However, in highlighting school choice policies like these, we want to reiterate that the nature of these agreements must be negotiated by specific national communities themselves and not imposed from above using a one-size-fits-all model. In this way, the autonomy of First Nations peoples will be respected to enable better responses to the unique contextual opportunities and challenges that exist within their communities.

Ethnic (immigrant) minority groups

In Chapter 3, we explored how schools, informed by the theory and principles of liberal multiculturalism, have been made more accommodating of and welcoming to ethnic minority groups. For example, schools with large Muslim populations have recognized Muslim holidays and created dedicated spaces for students to pray. Under a liberal multicultural matrix of understanding, these kinds of accommodations should be promoted and expanded to ensure that ethnic minority groups feel at home within the public education system. Accommodation of minority groups is balanced with the provision that individuals have *exit rights*, which ensure that individuals are not bound to attend a school based on their community of origin: "Positioning exit as a key right for members of minority groups seems to allow liberal democrats to maintain their endorsement of diversity while preserving their commitment to individual choice and self-authorship, autonomy, and freedom" (Ben-Porath, 2010, p. 121).

In this way, ethnic minority groups should not feel the need to opt out of the mainstream system and form institutionally separate schools, which would allow them to freely express their unique cultural identities. Accommodation with exit rights also allows for movement between communities of ethnicity or religion, such as for members who may decide to not enrol in schools based on identity factors. Although these types of accommodations have been introduced in many schools across Canada, calls by ethnocultural minority communities for separate heritage-language, Africentric, and faith-based schools have been met with varying support. In searching for principles that could guide policymakers in responding to these controversies, a liberal multicultural framework provides a clear set of policy guidelines for heritage-language and Africentric schools; however, this is not necessarily so for faith-based schools.

Heritage-language programs

As noted in Table 3, the western provinces have allowed public school districts to introduce a number of fully funded heritage-language schools where instruction occurs partly in an unofficial language (e.g., Mandarin, Ukrainian, German, Spanish, or Arabic). For instance, certain school districts in Manitoba offer fully funded English–Ukrainian, English–Hebrew, and English–German bilingual programs. Heritage-language schools are often situated in larger urban centres and offer only elementary-level instruction, after which students may enter either the French or the English education system. From a policy standpoint the key questions are, where numbers warrant, should ministries of education across Canada make policy provisions for bilingual heritage-language education, and should these programs be available from kindergarten through high school?

Critics of heritage-language school choice policies argue that immigrant groups are free to pass on their language to their children through private means; for example, by speaking their language with their children at home and enrolling their children in community-based language classes. However, the state must ensure that students learn one of the two official languages so they can integrate into Canadian society and fully participate in institutions that operate in French or English. This criticism reflects a belief that bilingual education programs delay or impede the acquisition of a dominant (national) language. From a liberal multicultural perspective, failing to fully learn one of the official languages would be problematic because it could lead to serious marginalization and disadvantage that could be passed on to the next generation (Kymlicka, 1998, p. 50). Thus, for policymakers guided by liberal multicultural perspectives to disallow the introduction of heritage-language programs, they would need to see empirical evidence to support the notion that heritage-language programs impede the acquisition of a dominant language.

A fairly substantial body of research currently indicates these concerns are largely unfounded. Recent studies suggest that heritage-language programs do not impede the acquisition of a dominant language. Rather, proficiency in the dominant language is actually increased when learners become proficient in their first language through heritage-language programs (Cummins, 2001; Lindholm-Leary, 2001; Macnab, 2010). Cummins (2001) found that second-language proficiency depends on proficiency in the students' first language. When children of immigrants do not receive sufficient heritage-language instruction, their competency in the official language is hindered. In addition, studies have also found that students enrolled in heritage-language programs have higher than normal levels of academic achievement (Thomas & Collier, 2002; Wu & Bilash, 2000). For instance, in Alberta, Wu and Bilash (2000) found that grade 3 and 6 students enrolled in heritage-language programs performed above average on provincial achievement tests in four subject areas, including English language arts. These tests are all delivered in English, which is notable given that only half of the students' instruction occurs in English.

Based on this research, a liberal multicultural framework would argue that bilingual heritage-language programs should be expanded in jurisdictions where they are already in place, and introduced in provinces and territories where they currently do not exist. However, in upholding the need to balance accommodations for cultural differences while also ensuring unity and social cohesion, a liberal multicultural framework would argue in favour of transitional heritage-language programs where the earliest years of education are conducted partly in the first language, leading to secondary and postsecondary education in either French or English (Kymlicka, 1998, p. 42).

Africentric schools

In the fall of 2013, Winston Churchill Collegiate in Scarborough, Ontario, opened the first Africentric program at a Canadian public high school (L. Brown, 2014). The purpose of this program was to support Black students who were disengaged and underperforming within the mainstream system. In the first year of operation, 19 students in grade 9 enrolled in the program. These students took core subjects together, but electives, such as physical education and drama, were taken with the greater student body. Open to all students regardless of their ethnic background, students enrolled in the program follow the Ontario curriculum; however, classroom lessons often draw on African- and Caribbean-themed resources more culturally relevant for the students. One of the teachers, who is Black, stated that "it's not so much about having all Black teachers ... You need teachers who are comfortable using materials that are more culturally diverse than what they're used to, and you don't have to be Black to do that" (L. Brown, 2014, para. 15).

Some advocates of this school program believed it offered a "progressive strategy to promote the academic achievement of 'failing' Black youth, while others saw it as a regressive step backward to the days of racial segregation" (Gordon & Zinga, 2012, pp. 1–2). Policymakers guided by the theory and practice of liberal multiculturalism would take the position that Africentric schools are acceptable as long as they are seen as a "transitional step aimed at reducing dropout rates and thereby enabling more Blacks to acquire the skills and credentials needed to succeed in the mainstream educational, economic, and political institutions in Canada" (Kymlicka, 1998, p. 84). Thus, rejecting the notion that Africentric schools promote racial segregation, the introduction of such a school or programming option would be seen as a means to reduce the likelihood that Black students, who feel alienated and are underachieving in the mainstream school system, begin to feel permanently separated from the greater society in ways that exist in numerous inner-city areas in the United States.

The need for educational jurisdictions that have significant populations of African Canadian students, including the Toronto District School Board, to explore provisions for Africentric schooling options is based on a substantial body of research that academic disengagement and dropout rates have been, and continue to be, a significant issue for Black youth (Gordon & Zinga, 2012; James & Brathwaite, 1996). For example, in the 2001 school year, the Toronto District School Board found that although students should have 16 credits by the time they reach grade 10, "54 percent of students born in the English-speaking Caribbean had 14 credits or fewer at the end of Grade 10" (as cited in Gordon & Zinga, 2012, p. 3). Whether introducing Africentric schools and programs would reduce this trend is open to debate, and more empirical research needs to be undertaken in this area (Dragnea & Erling, 2008). However, in the same way that Aboriginal students are often marginalized within the mainstream system, it is clear that significant challenges exist for African Canadian students in some educational contexts. Consequently, alongside greater efforts to reduce barriers for African Canadian students in mainstream education systems, policymakers should give Africentric schools serious consideration.

Faith-based schools

One of the most contentious educational policy issues in Canada today concerns the extent to which public education districts should provide partial or full funding for faith-based schools. During the 2007 Ontario election, for instance, Conservative party leader John Tory's proposal to fund faith-based schools became one of its most highly contested issues (J. Wilson, 2007). Critics of this policy position, including then Liberal minister of education Kathleen Wynne, took a strong stand against this proposal:

> (Ontarians) do not want to see our society divided. They do not want to see kids segregated from one another ... We need an inclusive system in this province that allows kids to learn together, be together and understand each other. (Gillespie, 2007, para. 7)

As can be seen in Wynne's remarks, critics of public funding for faith-based schools are concerned that they will promote cultural enclaves cut off from the diversity of the larger Canadian society. Many Ontarians voiced concerns that these schools might promote religiously sanctioned illiberal values that could be oppressive towards female students, for example. Ultimately, John Tory lost the election, leaving many to wonder if his policy position on this issue was at least partially to blame.

Constitutional provisions guarantee full funding for Catholic school boards in Ontario, Alberta, and Saskatchewan. In addition, as shown in Table 2, a number of provinces, including British Columbia, Alberta, Saskatchewan, Quebec, and Manitoba, have partial funding provisions for faith-based schools. For example, British Columbia provides from 35% to 50% funding for the Vancouver Hebrew Academy and the IQRA Islamic School in Surrey, which have met rigorous standards and teach the provincial curriculum. With these school choice models in place, policymakers have debated whether these provisions should be extended to other provincial and territorial jurisdictions and whether funding levels should be on par with mainstream schooling options.

As Kymlicka (2008) noted, much uncertainty remains about the place of faith-based schools within a liberal multicultural policy framework. While liberal multiculturalism provides clear guidelines and principles for addressing issues of ethnicity and race, "there are no comparable guidelines for how to deal with religious groups or faith-based claims" (p. 12). Kymlicka (2008) argued that multicultural frameworks would be able to address the issue of public funding for faith-based schools in much the same way as they have accommodated educational issues related to minority group culture and language rights. However, he contended that Canadians are only in the initial stages of this debate. Consequently, we turn to the work of liberal theory as outlined by Rawls (1993, 1999) to help guide policymakers in this school choice domain, with which all Western countries continue to struggle.

Liberal Theory and School Choice Policies

Though early school choice policies in Canada reflected a liberal multicultural perspective, this philosophical framework has been limited in its ability to provide a broader range of policy recommendations related to faith-based schools, alternative educational approaches to teaching and learning, or specialist schools that target a particular student demographic. We argue that liberal theory can fulfil this role because of its ability to move beyond purely ethnocultural considerations and attend to a diverse range of students' individual needs.

Contemporary liberal theory emphasizes "autonomy, individual rights, the freedom to develop and revise a life plan, and the need for civic education and a common political identity to provide unity in a diverse society" (Reich, 2002b, p. 3) as ideals to guide school choice policy. An interesting tension is at play here. As we noted in Chapter 1, on the one hand, liberal theorists suggest that the common school model is limited. By bringing a diverse array of students together under a common educational mandate, liberal theorists voice concerns that not all students will flourish in such a system. Yet on the other hand, a balancing act is required between individual interests and the broader civic responsibilities that diverse pluralistic societies require to ensure stability and social cohesion. In this way, liberals are attuned to the philosophical tension between the need for schools to foster autonomous adults while also promoting unity and a shared set of democratic values (Brighouse, 2000).

In attempting to mediate this tension, liberal theorists draw on the larger philosophical principle of ethical individualism to shift language commonly used in school choice debates away from the individual's *right to choose* towards consideration of what is required to ensure the individual's ability to flourish and live well within a democratic society. By asserting that the individual, rather than the group or state, should be the basic unit of analysis, under the principles of ethical individualism the state should "maintain a commitment to accommodating a wide range of visions of the good life as understood by individuals and expressed in their lives, activities, and affiliations" (Ben-Porath, 2010, p. 122). The need for such a stance is predicated on the reality that what it means to fulfil a good life or live well is contested, as there are plural and conflicting ideas of what this entails (Schrag, 1998).

By embracing diverse notions of the good life, the principles of ethical individualism affirm provisions for school choice based on the belief that no single, monolithic education system can attend to the range of needs, interests, and opportunities required for children to fully develop and flourish. Galston (2002) noted: "Deep diversity simply has intrinsic value since plural, conflicting values cannot all be harmonized within a single comprehensive way of life" (p. 27). Given this, we might assume that the principles of ethical individualism would then mandate that any school choice policy would suffice. This is not the case. As stated above, school choice policies guided by ethical individualism do not sanction choice for the sake of choice but as a means to provide alternative educational options for children that can foster and build their individual capacity for well-being.

Building on this point, a liberal stance on school choice policies must additionally attend to two other considerations. First, any provision for school choice cannot limit the autonomy of individual prospects. Specifically, a school choice policy might be denied if the educational mandate impedes individuals' ability to make informed judgments about how they want to lead their lives by limiting their exposure to alternative perspectives. Determining what is reasonable, unreasonable, and simply impermissible is, however, a difficult, value-laden task for policymakers. For Rawls (1985), policymakers might reject the introduction of specific schooling options if they do not adhere to the considerations of justice that inhibit "the basic essentials of a democratic regime" (p. 134). Rawls (1993) contended:

> If a comprehensive conception of the good is unable to endure in a society securing the familiar equal basic liberties and mutual toleration, there is no way to preserve it consistent with democratic values as expressed by the idea of society as a fair system of cooperation among citizens viewed as free and equal. (p. 198)

The second principle that guides provisions for school choice within liberal theory concerns the difference principle. According to Rawls (1999), the difference principle asserts that the opportunities of the least advantaged in society should be maximized. However, the difference principle is not a mechanism for giving all the resources to the poorest in a state; rather, the state has a responsibility to develop basic social structures that will ensure the highest possible standards for the least well off (Rawls, 1999). Under the difference principle, school choice policies should be introduced only if they do not further exacerbate economic disparities between rich and poor and, moreover, must actually be targeted to the least advantaged. Rawls (2001) wrote:

> Social and economic inequalities are to satisfy two conditions: first, they are to be attached to offices and positions open to all under conditions of fair equality of opportunity; and second, they are to be to the greatest benefit of the least-advantaged members of society (the difference principle). (pp. 42–43)

The difference principle is based on broader principles of distributive justice intended to indicate how to distribute the benefits and burdens of economic activity among individuals in a society. These principles may include the terms of income, wealth, opportunities, jobs, welfare, and utility; the nature of the recipients of the distribution; and the basis of how the distribution should be made. When we turn to the difference principle, the aim is to argue against a notion of strict equality whereby individuals are given the same resources. This fact is particularly relevant for school choice policies. Some accounts of educational equality invoke a notion of strict equality, which would mean that everyone would receive the same level of resources and services. Yet this is clearly disadvantageous for the diverse needs of students, given the cognitive, emotional, and social differences that may impede a student's abilities to do well in school. Thus, rather than making decisions based on notions of strict equality, those adhering to the difference principle argue as follows:

> If it is possible to raise the absolute position of the least advantaged further by having some inequalities of income and wealth, then the Difference Principle prescribes inequality up to that point where the absolute position of the least advantaged can no longer be raised. (Lamont & Favor, 2013, para. 21)

It is conceivable that while strict equality may not be attained, the application of the difference principle requires policymakers to consider whether the "distribution of education might in time lead to the worse off having more or better education than they would otherwise have and that this could itself yield important benefits" (Brighouse & Swift, 2008, p. 448). In this way, the difference principle attempts to address a potential levelling down that could occur if a strict notion of educational equality were employed, which may create fewer opportunities or diminished opportunities for students to flourish. Conversely, the aim is to consider how the least advantaged members might fare better despite unequal distribution of social or economic equality.

Based on these tenets of liberal theory, diverse school choice options become available that are more far-reaching than what can be provided under Kymlicka's (1998, 2007) liberal multicultural framework. To demonstrate this, we consider three key areas that would benefit under liberal theory: faith-based schools, alternative educational philosophies for teaching and learning, and schools that cater to specific learning needs. We also consider two areas in need of additional monitoring: home-schooling and elite specialist schools.

Faith-based schools

As noted at the end of the first section, provisions for faith-based schooling in Canada remain contested. It is clear that faith-based schools acknowledge and support individuals' and families' faith under a notion of deep diversity. In this way, faith-based schools can be considered a viable school choice option. This being said, although the introduction of faith-based schools attends to the diverse perspectives of individuals within society, it also raises concerns that particular faith-based schools may not expose students to alternative perspectives. In principle then, following the theorizing of Rawls's (1993, 1999) liberal framework, faith-based schools can be considered one of many school choice options so long as they do not limit students' exposure to alternative world views that could help them become autonomous individuals able to pursue their individual well-being.

Provision of faith-based schools can be seen in varying contexts both within and beyond public education systems in Canada, most notably with Jewish, Islamic, Hutterite, and Christian schools. Limitations on faith-based educational options in Canada centre on the principle that such schools curtail student autonomy and go against broader liberal democratic values. For instance, in R. v. Jones (1986), a fundamentalist Christian preacher (Jones) had been teaching his and other children in a church basement in Alberta. Jones did not want his children being taught in a mainstream school and instead sought to educate them himself. The Supreme Court of Canada rejected Jones's claims that the School Act served "to foster religious freedom in the education of its citizens rather than curtail it" (R. v. Jones, 1986, para. 51). Justice L.A. Forest, speaking on behalf of the majority, noted that "it should not be forgotten that the state, too, has an interest in the education of its citizens" (R. v. Jones, 1986, para. 51).

In the Supreme Court's decision, we can see the application of liberal principles. Rights at the individual level are acknowledged but within limits. First, school choice provisions must not limit an individual's prospects because of a lack of exposure to alternative perspectives on how to lead his or her life. Second, the schooling must not limit broader civic responsibilities within a democratic society. The Supreme Court felt that the preacher violated both of these principles.

A number of religious schools in Canada have drawn on liberal discourse to advocate for their full or partial funding, such as the Logos school in Edmonton. Its supporters, to secure funding for the school, employed a legal discourse of minority rights, "suggesting that Christians were 'oppressed by a secular and intolerant majority'" (A. Taylor & Mackay, 2008, p. 557). This is a difficult argument for school boards and provincial and territorial governments to refute, as the Canadian Charter of Rights and Freedoms protects against discrimination based on religion. Furthermore, advocates of religious schools have noted that a number of provinces already fund Catholic schools, so why should other religions be excluded?

In response, some school districts, such as the Edmonton Public School Board, have avoided creating a clear policy on this matter. For example, a district representative of the board stated, "'We don't have a lot of clear definition in policy' about how alternative programs are established. He adds that 'it was almost a policy to have no policy' in order to have flexibility" (A. Taylor & Mackay, 2008, p. 557). This quote suggests that some policymakers have avoided relying on a larger set of philosophical principles to make decisions in relation to faith-based schools. However, with increasing calls for public funding for faith-based schools, the absence of such principles within jurisdictions that already provide partial or full funding for some faith-based schools may not be tenable in the long term.

Alternative philosophical school choice options

Under a liberal framework, school choice options can be offered when the alternative educational mandate is not currently provided in public schools and would enhance the development and learning of the child. Offering schooling options for students and parents that draw on different theories of learning allows for an array of educational values. Most commonly, alternative schooling programs follow a particular philosophy or orientation to teaching and learning that defines the school culture and approach to the organization and delivery of the mandated program of study, as well as supplemental curricular offerings. Examples of these alternative schooling options offered by many school jurisdictions in Canada include Montessori (American Montessori Society, 2015), Waldorf (Steiner, 1919/1985), Summerhill-inspired democratic schools (Vaughan, 2006), and Reggio Emilia (Hewitt, 2001).

The inclusion of various schooling options aligns well with a liberal theoretical framework in that it affirms no singular dominant approach to learning and teaching; rather, a deep diversity of pedagogical perspectives parallel different ways of learning. For example, Montessori education provides a school choice option that emphasizes independence, freedom within limits, and respect for a child's natural, psychological, physical, and social development (American Montessori Society, 2015). A publically funded Waldorf schooling option provides a humanistic approach to pedagogy that emphasizes the integration of intellectual, practical, and artistic activities across the curriculum, towards developing morally responsible children and youth with a strong sense of social responsibility (Steiner, 1919/1985).

Special needs programs

Programs that educate students with special needs and attend to their individual differences in congregated rather than inclusive settings are another school option that a liberal theory would promote. For instance, it is relatively uncontested that schools that attend to the Deaf may better serve the needs of their students in a much more effective way. Cummins (2009) noted that "the devaluation of community languages (e.g. American Sign Language in the case of the Deaf community) in the wider society results in ambivalence among parents and educators about whether these languages should be strongly supported in home and school" (p. 261). Generally, educators and policymakers attempt to support students within an inclusive environment in a regular classroom. As such, there is a need for a continuum of placement options and support services to accommodate particular needs (Ambrose, Sternberg, & Sriraman, 2012; Kalambouka, Farrell, Dyson, & Kaplan, 2007; Katz, 2012; Slee, 2011).

Special needs programs can be authorized so long as the school provides evidence to suggest how the program will meet the needs of students who are not currently well served and unable to flourish under current circumstances. The argument in favour of allowing special needs programs and schools is based on the liberal notion that students would be more likely to thrive because the staff have particular areas of expertise to fully support them. The kinds of schools that might be offered in this category range from ones that serve students with specific emotional or behavioural needs, gifted students who may not be challenged or may underachieve because of specific learning needs, and students with significant cognitive or developmental needs that may be better supported by specialist teachers.

Limitations of school choice provisions within liberal theory

Within this expansive range of school choice provisions that liberal theory supports are some limitations. In what follows, we note some of these restrictions, as well as areas that would require more regulations and monitoring before school choice policies for particular types of schooling could be endorsed.

HOMESCHOOLING

Liberal theorists tend to take a cautionary stance towards provisions for homeschooling, for reasons similar to those discussed for limits to faith-based schooling (Kunzman, 2012; Reich, 2002a). Central to this stance is the fact that the "state's interest in educating children for life in a pluralist democracy trumps any asserted parental liberty interest in controlling their children's education" (Ross, 2010, p. 991). Along these lines, liberal theorists argue for appropriate limitations on parental control over children's education to mitigate children being exposed to extreme forms of illiberal homeschooling (Yuracko, 2008, p. 189). They would not overtly deny the provision of homeschooling but would approve it *only* where clear regulatory and monitoring mechanisms ensure the education provided does not impede the child's development into an autonomous individual capable of participating in democratic society (Basham, Merrifield, & Hepburn, 2007; Davies & Aurini, 2003; Glenn, 2015).

Generally, the provision for homeschooling can be endorsed only if it meets certain requirements. First, families must register their children with a local school authority to ensure that there is a record of students being homeschooled in a particular jurisdiction. Second, families must follow the approved program of studies to ensure that students receive a range of perspectives so as to not limit their personal autonomy or future opportunities as adults. Finally, school authorities must regularly monitor student progress to ensure that the homeschooling meets the local school authorities' expectations. Failure to meet these requirements may compromise the education provided by the family to adequately meet the learning needs of the child. While the lack of monitoring is prominent in some localities in the United States (Reich, 2005), this appears to be less of a concern in Canada (Davies & Aurini, 2003).

ELITE SPECIALIST SCHOOLS

Generally, liberal theorists would hesitate to allow school choice options for elite academies, including sports or fine and performing arts schools, based on the belief that such schools further the advantage of a particular group of students to the disadvantage of others. Liberal theorists argue elite specialist schools exacerbate the positional advantages accrued by families who have the ability to build capacity for their children through extracurricular and tutorial support (Swift, 2003). Similarly, liberals tend to caution that such specialist schools will have extra fees that may hinder students from disadvantaged backgrounds from enrolling in the program. For instance, an elite sports school caters to students who may have special talent but also have access to the extracurricular activities and coaching to support the development of their talent. This situation intensifies the divide between families who can afford to pay for these extra costs outside of school and families who cannot. However, a specialist school, such as a sports or performing arts school, could be endorsed based on the difference principle *if* it was placed in a neighbourhood that could be accessed by underprivileged children who would normally not have the opportunity to experience such activities.

In making such a decision, policymakers could choose whether to endorse the specialist school based on responses to the following questions:

1 Who is eligible to apply to the specialist school?
2 Are there additional costs associated with attending the school?
3 Does the school target disadvantaged children?
4 Does the school provide bursaries to children who could not attend for financial reasons?

Guided by liberal theory, responding to these questions would help policymakers ensure that the school does not further advantage some children and disadvantage children from low-income families. Without this assurance, liberals would not endorse such schools.

Neoliberalism and School Choice Policies

Unlike the two philosophical perspectives already explored in this chapter that attend to accommodations for ethnocultural diversity and better meeting the needs of individual children within the parameters of a pluralist society, neoliberalism starts from an economic premise (Chubb & Moe, 1990; Friedman, 1962). Building on our examination in Chapter 1, neoliberalism suggests that market-based principles will create conditions for higher quality schooling options for all students if the following three elements are introduced: (1) deregulation of the educational system to increase provisions for parental choice (Chubb & Moe, 1990), (2) fiscal accountability largely determined by allowing educational funding to follow children to their school of choice (Lawton, 2001), and (3) metrics that hold schools accountable for improved student achievement (Holmes, 1998).

Recent developments in education reform (1990s to early 2000s) have included expanded school choice provisions inspired by neoliberal principles that include standards-based accountability and market-based competition as evidenced in Alberta (A. Taylor, 2001b), British Columbia (Fallon & Paquette, 2008), and Ontario (Gidney, 1999). The clearest example of neoliberal ideology driving reform in Canada can be found in Alberta. In 1994, Alberta Premier Ralph Klein unveiled an education reform strategy that introduced charter school legislation, increased funding to private schools, initiated standards-based accountability through provincial standardized testing and diploma examinations, consolidated school boards, and created mechanisms for more parental voice through parent-based school councils (Bruce & Schwartz, 1997).

Premier Klein summed up his vision of education reform as follows:

> It is an education system that demands high standards, and is monitored through detailed performance measurement: a system that gives more say to the teacher and the parent, and less to the administrator; a system that ensures equitable funding for a student regardless of where he or she lives in Alberta; and an education that guarantees a student an equal opportunity, not an equal outcome. In short, we are building an education system that will make our kids better prepared, to be more competitive, in a world that demands excellence. (as quoted in A. Taylor, 2001b, p. 72)

These ideals parallel the prominent neoliberal education agenda propagated during the 1990s in the United States, the United Kingdom, and New Zealand. Inherent in this agenda is increased parental voice and authority to choose schools and more explicit forms of accountability and performance metrics to measure educational quality. Through processes of competition and choice, a neoliberal education agenda assumes that market demand will ensure quality education of benefit to all children and that parents are best equipped to choose the kind of education most suited for their child. With parents demanding better schooling options, schools would need to raise the quality of the education provided to students, or families would vote with their feet (Cyre & Fyre, 2004). School choice provisions within a neoliberal framework aim to address the needs and demands of parents not well served within the current system and to increase pressure on schools that are not providing a quality education to improve student achievement or close because of low enrolment. It is hoped that the economic principles of supply and demand, together with accountability and achievement, will inject healthy competition among schools otherwise perceived as stagnant or mediocre.

Given that neoliberalism draws from market-based principles to guide policy decisions, it lacks a traditional ethical basis to justify school choice provisions. Specifically, the evaluative component of school choice provisions within a neoliberal framework does not necessarily focus on accommodations for particular groups. While neoliberalism does arguably focus on the individual child, it does so not to increase the child's future opportunities or autonomy but rather to respond to parental (consumer) demand for particular school choice options (Norris, 2011). From a policy perspective, this has interesting implications. If a proposal is brought forth to create an alternative choice school based on parental demand, it could be approved so long as it meets student achievement benchmarks and is fiscally accountable. Acceptable levels of student achievement are measured by (1) school performance on standardized achievement tests (SATs) ranked and compared with other schools in the district and (2) a demonstrable increase in individual student performance from the previous school to the choice school. Commonly, fiscal accountability is measured by student enrolment, balanced budgets, and financial sustainability, as is the case with Alberta public charter schools (Alberta Education, 1996).

If a school cannot demonstrate increased student achievement or fiscal accountability, then a neoliberal framework would necessitate its closure. While fiscal mismanagement metrics are fairly straightforward, closure based on low levels of student achievement is more complex and contingent on the school mandate and student population it serves. In the case of charter schools, little conclusive evidence from US studies suggests that charter schools are boosting academic achievement in a significant or sustained manner (Berends, Goldring, Stein, & Cravens, 2010; Lubienski, 2012; Ravitch, 2010; Smith, Wohlstetter, Farrell, & Nayfack, 2011). This lack of support is partly attributed to problems in designing robust research to track students, determining the appropriate group to compare charter school outcomes, and deciding whether student achievement can be attributed to innovative teaching practices, student selection, the culture of the school, or a combination of factors (Bosetti & Butterfield, 2015).

Not all charter schools, however, see increasing academic achievement as one of their primary aims. Boyle Street Education Centre, a charter school in Edmonton, is one example. Its focus is to engage marginalized youth who may be living on the street, have dropped out, or have been expelled from school. Specifically, the school seeks to help this demographic obtain a skill set that will help them transition to the workforce and find stability in their lives. This school illustrates the limitations of a market-based accountability scheme to meet the needs of all students. Some marginalized populations, such as students at Boyle Street Education Centre, do not have parent advocates to demand programs to address their needs, nor are they motivated to attend school or to be recruited by specialist choice programs.

Another limitation of school choice provisions within a neoliberal framework concerns the metrics of financial viability. Students who have higher than normal learning needs would require equity-based funding to receive resources to facilitate their learning. Simply put, they are more expensive to educate. Neoliberal principles are insufficient to guide policymakers in the equitable distribution of resources. For example, a high demand may exist for a school that serves the cultural and English-language learning needs of immigrant students, but without equity funding, the school may not have adequate resources to support these learners and improve their achievement on standardized tests. These can become ghettoized neighbourhood schools abandoned by motivated parents and students for more supportive, resource-rich school environments. The question becomes, is it reasonable to close a neighbourhood school that is left with low-achieving students? Or does this school have an obligation to provide additional resources to support the success of those students left behind?

In competitive educational markets, schools may find ways to screen out difficult and hard-to-teach students with behavioural issues, learning disabilities, and disengaged parents. Ultimately, provisions for school choice within a neoliberal framework are not based on an ethical or pedagogical rationale; rather, they are based on consumer demand and demonstrated success in measuring up to various regimes of accountability. Given the underlying economic principles that inform school choice policies within a neoliberal framework, we contend that these principles provide an insufficient basis from which to guide school choice policies.

Conclusion

When policymakers design parameters for school choice, they must consider the underlying philosophical principles that guide such decisions. Throughout this chapter, we have argued that both liberal multiculturalism and elements of liberalism provide a way to address ethnocultural diversity in Canadian society, as well as policy decisions related to faith-based schools, alternative educational approaches to teaching and learning, and specialist schools targeting a particular student demographic. In making this argument, we believe that the promise of school choice to improve the quality of education for all children will not be achieved through market forces alone. Parameters for choice in schooling options must take into consideration educational and social aims (equalized access and opportunity) that ensure the most disadvantaged children are accommodated, including those who are poor, come from marginalized groups, and possess learning challenges. When considered, "policy makers can change institutional arrangements and shape alternative structures and incentives for school, and schools can respond to those factors in how they organize themselves and arrange their resources" (Lubienski, 2012, p. 154). However, it is important to note that without change in the quality of education and instructional practice at the classroom level, school choice policies will have a limited impact on increased student achievement (P. Hill, 2010; Lubienski, 2003, 2012).

To summarize, the following principles can help policymakers when considering provisions for school choice:

1 Within a liberal multicultural framework (Kymlicka, 1998, 2007), school choice policies targeting national minority groups in Canada should work to create educational conditions where francophone and Aboriginal peoples gain a level of institutional separateness so they can sustain themselves as distinct linguistic and cultural communities.
2 A liberal multicultural approach to school choice policies would be in favour of introducing or increasing the number of primary and elementary bilingual non-official language programs because little empirical evidence suggests that heritage-language programs impede the acquisition of a dominant language (Kymlicka, 1998, 2007). However, based on the need to balance the need to respect minority group languages while ensuring unity and social cohesion, children in these programs would transition to either French or English schools at the secondary and postsecondary levels.
3 A liberal multicultural framework (Kymlicka, 1998, 2007) would include a strong argument to introduce schools targeting one specific ethnic group, such as Africentric schools. For students from a particular ethnic background who feel alienated and discriminated against, and who are underachieving in the mainstream school system, such schools can offer the best chance to gain the confidence, positive sense of self, and skills needed to succeed in mainstream educational, political, and economic institutions.
4 At this time, liberal multiculturalism (Kymlicka, 1998, 2007) provides little guidance concerning state funding for faith-based schools. However, within Rawls's (1993, 1999) liberal framework, faith-based schools, as well as provisions for homeschooling, can be considered as long as they do not promote extreme forms of illiberal beliefs and limit students' exposure to alternative world views that could help them become autonomous individuals able to pursue their individual well-being.
5 Under a liberal framework (Rawls, 1993, 1999), school choice options for alternative schooling programs, including Montessori schools and schools that serve special needs populations, can be offered when evidence indicates that the alternative educational

mandate is not currently provided in public schools and would enhance the development and learning of the child.

6 Generally, liberal theorists (Rawls, 1993, 1999) would not allow school choice options for elite academies, including sports or performing arts schools, based on the belief that such schools further benefit already advantaged students to the disadvantage of other students. However, these schools could be considered if they are accessible to all students, do not require any additional costs, and provide provisions for disadvantaged children.

7 School choice policies guided by a neoliberal framework are highly problematic for a host of reasons. For instance, the need for schools to show financial competitiveness would most likely lead to avoid admitting students with higher than normal learning needs because of the extra resources and supports that these students would require.

For school choice policies to be effective, a balance needs to provide some flexibility for educators and policymakers in responding to various educational mandates that may benefit a particular group of students while considering the impacts both to those students who enrol in some alternative provision of education and the potential implications for those students external to that school. The general rule should be that while some students may be better off attending an alternative program, those students left behind should not be worse off. In other words, a kind of balancing act is required where robust school choice policies enhance broader public education rather than threaten or undermine the public system. Government cannot take a hands-off approach but must provide the parameters and financial supports in which school choice policies align and complement neighbourhood schools and enhance the quality of education for all students.

It is clear that the political debate regarding school choice policies will not go away in Canadian education. How school choice policy is shaped by the political landscape, however, is very much in the hands of educators and policymakers. We have argued that egalitarian principles can inform policy, and we suggest that market-based approaches may be ill conceived in the short and long term. The task to delineate better and worse applications for alternative options in education can be guided by considerations of the democratic ideal in terms of equality of opportunity and the difference principle. This delineation often means that school choice must be properly supported financially to allow access and opportunities to those families commonly unable to pursue these educational options.

References

Aboriginal Affairs and Northern Development Canada. (2008a). *First nation education partnership and agreements.* Retrieved from https://www.aadnc-aandc .gc.ca/eng/1308840098023/1308840148639

Aboriginal Affairs and Northern Development Canada. (2008b). *Partnership and agreements.* Retrieved from https://www.aadnc-aandc.gc.ca/eng/ 1308840098023/1308840148639

Aboriginal Affairs and Northern Development Canada. (2008c). *Statement of apology: Prime Minster Harper offers full apology on behalf of Canadians for the Indian residential schools system.* Retrieved from http://www.aadnc-aandc.gc.ca/ eng/1100100015644/1100100015649

Aboriginal Affairs and Northern Development Canada. (2012). *Developing a First Nation education act: A discussion guide.* Retrieved from https://www .aadnc-aandc.gc.ca/DAM/DAM-INTER-HQ-EDU/STAGING/texte-text/ edu_dfnea_guide_1355149831546_eng.pdf

Adler v. *Ontario,* [1996] 3 SCR, 609.

Alberta Education. (1996). *Charter school handbook.* Edmonton, AB: Author.

Alberta Education. (2006). *Home education regulations.* Retrieved from http:// education.alberta.ca/parents/choice/homeeducation.aspx

Alberta Education. (2009). *Charter school concept paper: Consideration of a vision for the future of charter schools.* Retrieved from http://www.education.alberta .ca/media/6389633/abed_charterschoolconceptpaper_web%20pdf.pdf

Alberta Education. (2010). *Inspiring education: A dialogue with Albertans.* Edmonton, AB: Author.

Alberta Education. (2011a). *Charter school handbook.* Retrieved from http:// education.alberta.ca/media/434258/charter_hndbk.pdf

Alberta Education. (2011b). *Framework for student learning: Competencies for engaged thinking and ethical citizens with an entrepreneurial spirit.* Retrieved from http://education.alberta.ca/media/6581166/framework.pdf

Alberta Education. (2012). *Historical overview.* Retrieved from https://
    education.alberta.ca/francais/admin/immersion/handbookimm/
    01approach/histoverview.aspx

Alberta Teachers' Association. (2011). *Initial response to action on research and
    innovation: The future of charter schools in Alberta.* Edmonton, AB: Author.

Allison, D., & Van Pelt, D. (2012). Canada. In C. Glenn & J. De Groof (Eds.),
    Balancing freedom, autonomy and accountability in education (2nd ed., Vol. 3,
    pp. 79–146). Nijmegen, The Netherlands: Wolf Legal.

Alpha Alternative School. (2015). *About ALPHA.* Retrieved from http://
    alphaschool.ca/about/

Alphonso, C., & Maki, A. (2014, January 8). Math wrath: Parents and teachers
    demanding a return to basic skills. *The Globe and Mail.* Retrieved from http://
    www.theglobeandmail.com/news/national/education/petitions-press-
    provinces-to-put-emphasis-on-basic-math-skills/article16240118/

Ambrose, D., Sternberg, R., & Sriraman, B. (2012). Considering the effects
    of dogmatism on giftedness and talent development. In D. Ambrose, R.
    Sternberg, & B. Sriraman (Eds.), *Confronting dogmatism in gifted education*
    (pp. 3–10). New York, NY: Routledge.

American Montessori Society (2015). *Introduction to Montessori.* Retrieved from
    http://amshq.org/Montessori%20Education/Introduction%20to%
    20Montessori.

Amiskwaciy Academy (n.d.). *Instructional focus.* Retrieved from http://
    amiskwaciy.epsb.ca/aboutourschool/instructionalfocus/

Andre-Bechely, L. (2005). Public school choice at the intersection of voluntary
    integration and not-so-good neighborhood schools: Lessons from parents'
    experiences. *Educational Administration Quarterly, 41*(2), 267–305. http://
    dx.doi.org/10.1177/0013161X04269593

Arneson, R. (1999). Against Rawlsian equality of opportunity. *Philosophical
    Studies, 93*(1), 77–112. http://dx.doi.org/10.1023/A:1004270811433

Arthur, J. (with Bailey, R.). (2000). *Schools and community: The communitarian
    agenda in education.* London, England: Falmer Press.

Assembly of First Nations. (2010). *First Nations control of First Nations education:
    It's our vision, it's our time.* Retrieved from http://www.afn.ca/uploads/files/
    education/3._2010_july_afn_first_nations_control_of_first_nations_
    education_final_eng.pdf

Assembly of First Nations. (2012). *Assembly of First Nations: Education, jurisdiction,
    and governance: Cultural competency report.* Retrieved from http://www.afn.ca/
    uploads/files/education/8.1.pdf

Association of Independent Schools and Colleges in Alberta. (2008). *Funded
    enrolment trends in independent schools.* Retrieved from http://www.aisca.ab.ca/
    enrolments.html

Aurini, J., & Davies, S. (2005). Choice without markets: Homeschooling in the context of private education. *British Journal of Sociology of Education, 26*(4), 461–74. http://dx.doi.org/10.1080/01425690500199834

Avis, J. (2003). Re-thinking trust in a performative culture: The case of education. *Journal of Education Policy, 18*(3), 315–32. http://dx.doi.org/10.1080/02680930305577

Bains, R. (2014). *Myths and realities of First Nations education.* Vancouver, BC: The Fraser Institute Centre for Aboriginal Policy Studies. Retrieved from https://www.fraserinstitute.org/sites/default/files/myths-and-realities-of-first-nations-education.pdf

Ball, D. (2007). *Programs of choice and school culture* (Unpublished master's thesis). University of Calgary, Calgary, Alberta, Canada.

Ball, D., & Lund, D. (2010). School choice, school culture, and social justice: A Canadian case study. *Journal of Contemporary Issues in Education, 5*(2), 36–52. Retrieved from http://ejournals.library.ualberta.ca/index.php/JCIE/article/view/9974

Ball, S. (2003). *Class strategies and the education market: The middle classes and social advantage.* London, England: RoutledgeFalmer. http://dx.doi.org/10.4324/9780203218952

Ball, S. (2007). *Education PLC: Understanding private sector participation in public sector education.* London, England: Routledge.

Barlow, M., & Robertson, H. (1994). *Class warfare: The assault on Canada's schools.* Toronto, ON: Key Porter Books.

Basham, P., & Hepburn, C. (2001). Home schooling is an effective alternative to the public school system. *Public Policy Sources, 51.* Retrieved from http://oldfraser.lexi.net/publications/pps/51/homeschool.pdf

Basham, P., Merrifield, J., & Hepburn, C. (2007). *Home schooling: From extreme to mainstream* (2nd ed.). Vancouver, BC: Fraser Institute; Retrieved from https://www.fraserinstitute.org/sites/default/files/Homeschooling2007.pdf

Bauch, P.A., & Goldring, E.B. (1995). Parent involvement and school responsiveness: Facilitating the home–school connection in schools of choice. *Educational Evaluation and Policy Analysis, 17*(1), 1–21. Retrieved from http://www.jstor.org/stable/1164267

Belfield, C.R., & Levin, H. (2002). The effects of competition between schools on educational outcomes: A review of United States. *Review of Educational Research, 72*(2), 279–341. http://dx.doi.org/10.3102/00346543072002279

Bell, D., Anderson, K., Fortin, T., Ottmann, J., Rose, S., Simard, L., & Spencer, K. (2004). *Sharing our success: Ten case studies in aboriginal schooling.* Kelowna, BC: Society for the Advancement of Excellence in Education.

Ben-Porath, S. (2009). School choice as a bounded ideal. *Journal of Philosophy of Education, 43*(4), 527–44. http://dx.doi.org/10.1111/j.1467-9752.2009.00726.x

Ben-Porath, S. (2010). *Tough choices: Structured paternalism and the landscape of choice.* Princeton, NJ: Princeton University Press. http://dx.doi.org/10.1515/9781400836864

Berends, M., Goldring, E., Stein, M., & Cravens, X. (2010). *Instructional conditions in charter schools and students' mathematics achievement gains* (Research brief, National Centre on School Choice). Retrieved from http://files.eric.ed.gov/fulltext/ED511727.pdf

Bosetti, L. (1998a). *Canada's charter schools: Initial report.* Kelowna, BC: Society for the Advancement of Excellence in Education.

Bosetti, L. (1998b). The dark promise of charter schools. *Policy Options, 29*(6), 63–67.

Bosetti, L. (2000). Alberta charter schools: Paradox and promise. *Alberta Journal of Educational Research, 46*(2), 179–90. Retrieved from http://ajer.journalhosting.ucalgary.ca/index.php/ajer/article/view/205

Bosetti, L. (2001). The charter school experience. In C. Hepburn (Ed.), *Can the markets save our schools?* (pp. 101–20). Vancouver, BC: Fraser Institute.

Bosetti, L. (2004). Determinants of school choice: Understanding how parents choose elementary schools. *Journal of Education Policy, 19*(4), 387–405. http://dx.doi.org/10.1080/0268093042000227465

Bosetti, L. (2005). School choice: Public education at a crossroad. *American Journal of Education, 111*(4), 435–41. http://dx.doi.org/10.1086/431179

Bosetti, L., & Butterfield, P. (2015). *The politics of educational reform: The Alberta charter school experiment 20 years later.* Paper presented at Canadian Society for the Study of Education, University of Ottawa, Ottawa, June 4.

Bosetti, L., & Pyryt, M. (2007). Parental motivation in school choice: Seeking the competitive edge. [Special Issue]. *Journal of School Choice, 1*(4), 89–108. http://dx.doi.org/10.1300/15582150802098795

Bouchard, G. (2001). Nation et co-intégration contre la pensée dichotomique. [Nation and cointegration against dichotomous thinking] In J. Maclure & A. Gagnon (Eds.), *Repères en mutation: Identité et citoyenneté dans le Québec contemporain.* [Changing landmarks: Identity and citizenship in contemporary Quebec] (pp. 21–36). Montreal, QC: Québec Amérique.

Bouchard, G., & Taylor, C. (2008). *Building the Future: A Time for Reconciliation. The Consultation Commission on Accommodation Practices Related to Cultural Differences (CCAPRCD) Final Teport.* Retrieved from https://www.mce.gouv.qc.ca/publications/CCPARDC/rapport-final-integral-en.pdf

Boudreault, F.-A., Haga, J., Paylor, B., Sabourin, A., Thomas, S., & van der Linden, C. (2013). *Future tense: Adapting Canadian education systems for the 21st century.* Retrieved from http://www.actioncanada.ca/project/future-tense-adapting-canadian-education-systems-21st-century

Bourdieu, P. (1986). The forms of capital. In J. Richardson (Ed.), *Handbook of theory and research for the sociology of education* (pp. 241–58). New York, NY: Greenwood Press.

Bourdieu, P., & Boltanski, L. (1978). Changes in social structure and changes in the demand for education. In S. Giner & M. Archer (Eds.), *Contemporary Europe: Social structure and cultural change* (pp. 197–227). London, England: Routledge and Kegan Paul.

Bowles, W., & Jensen, M. (2001). *MIMO (more in more out): A socio-economic model for the 21st century.* Retrieved from http://www.williambowles.info/mimo/index.htm

Brighouse, H. (2000). *School choice and social justice.* Oxford, England: Oxford University Press.

Brighouse, H. (2004). What's wrong with privatising schools? *Journal of Philosophy of Education, 38*(4), 617–31. http://dx.doi.org/10.1111/j.0309-8249.2004.00408.x

Brighouse, H., & Swift, A. (2008). Putting educational equality in its place. *Education Finance and Policy, 3*(4), 444–66. http://dx.doi.org/10.1162/edfp.2008.3.4.444

British Columbia Ministry of Education (2009). *Alternative education program.* Retrieved from http://www2.gov.bc.ca/gov/content/education-training/administration/legislation-policy/public-schools/alternate-education-program

British Columbia Ministry of Education. (2013). *How are we doing? Aboriginal performance data.* Victoria, BC: Author.

British Columbia Ministry of Education. (2014). *French immersion program.* Retrieved from http://www2.gov.bc.ca/gov/topic.page?id=DCBD126F605646F7B16D62E5D09CD289

British Columbia Ministry of Education. (2015). *BC education plan: Focus on learning.* Retrieved from http://www.bcedplan.ca/

Brochu, P., Deussing, M.-A., Houme, K., & Chuy, M. (2013). *Measuring up: Canadian results of the OECD PISA study: The performance of Canada's youth in mathematics, reading and science: 2012 first results for Canadians aged 15.* Toronto, Canada: Council of Ministers of Education.

Brown, L. (2014, February 26). Africentric high school students thrive in pioneering program. *Toronto Star.* Retrieved from http://www.thestar.com/yourtoronto/education/2014/02/26/africentric_high_school_students_thrive_in_pioneering_program.html

Brown, P. (1997). The "third wave": Education and ideology of parentocracy. In A.H. Halsey, H. Lauder, P. Brown, & A.S. Wells (Eds.), *Education, culture, economy and society* (pp. 393–408). Oxford, England: Oxford University Press.

Brown, P. (2000). Globalisation of positional competition? *Sociology, 34*(4), 633–53. http://dx.doi.org/10.1017/S0038038500000390

Bruce, C., & Schwartz, A. (1997). Education: Meeting the challenge. In K. McKenzie (Ed.), *A government re-invented* (pp. 383–416). Toronto, ON: Oxford.

Bruner, J.S. (1963). *The process of education.* Cambridge, MA: Harvard University Press.

Canada History. (2013). *Pierre Elliot Trudeau: Multiculturalism.* Retrieved from http://www.canadahistory.com/sections/documents/Primeministers/trudeau/docs-onmulticulturalism.htm

Canadian Education Association. (2015). *In Nova Scotia, a Mi'kmaw model for First Nation education.* Retrieved from http://www.cea-ace.ca/education-canada/article/nova-scotia-mi'kmaw-model-first-nation-education

Canadian Parents for French. (2010). *The state of French-second-language education in Canada 2010: Executive summary.* Retrieved from http://cpf.ca/en/files/2010-FSL-Report4.pdf

Canadiana. (2015). *Acts of the parliament of the Dominion of Canada relating to criminal law and to procedure in criminal cases: Passed in the 2nd, 3rd, and 4th sessions of the third parliament.* Retrieved from http://eco.canadiana.ca/view/oocihm.9_02041/56?r=0&s=1

Canadians for 21st Century Learning & Innovation. (2012). *Shifting minds 3.0: A 21st century vision of public education in Canada.* Retrieved from http://www.c21canada.org/c21-research/

Carson, T. (2006). Help without giving advice: Pinar, curriculum studies and Canada. *Curriculum Teaching and Dialogue, 8*(1/2), 185–92.

Centre for Research and Information on Canada. (2002). *The charter: Uniting or dividing Canadians?* Retrieved from www.library.carleton.ca/sites/default/files/find/.../cric-crf-02-not.pdf

Chen, S. (2010). *Segregation versus self-determination: A black and white debate on Canada's first Africentric school* (Unpublished master's thesis). University of Toronto, Canada.

Chiefs Assembly on Education. (2012). *A portrait of First Nations and education.* Retrieved from http://www.afn.ca/uploads/files/events/fact_sheet-ccoe-3.pdf

Chubb, J., & Moe, T. (1990). *Politics, markets and America's schools.* Washington, DC: The Brookings Institute.

Clark, P. (2004). The historical context of social studies in English Canada. In A. Sears & I. Wright (Eds.), *Challenges and prospects for Canadian social studies* (pp. 17–37). Vancouver, BC: Pacific Educational Press.

Clemens, J., Palacios, M., Loyer, J., & Fathers, F. (2014). *Measuring choice and competition in Canadian education: An update on school choice in Canada.* Vancouver, BC: Barbara Mitchell Centre for Improvement in Education (Fraser Institute).

Coleman, J.S. (1988). Social capital in the creation of human capital. *American Journal of Sociology*, *94*(s1), S95–S120. Retrieved from http://dx.doi.org/10.1086/228943

Collins, R. (1979). *The credential society: An historical sociology of education and stratification.* New York, NY: Academic Press.

Corporate Higher-Learning Forum. (1990). *To be our best: Learning for the future.* Montreal, QC: Corporate-Higher Learning Forum.

Coulson, A. (2009). Comparing public, private and market schools: The international evidence. *Journal of School Choice*, *3*(1), 31–54. http://dx.doi.org/10.1080/15582150902805016

Cummins, J. (2001). Linguistic interdependence and the educational development of bilingual children. In J. Cummins, C. Baker, & N.H. Hornberger (Eds.), *An introductory reader to the writings of Jim Cummins* (pp. 63–95). Clevedon, UK: Multilingual Matters.

Cummins, J. (2009). Pedagogies of choice: Challenging coercive relations of power in classrooms and communities. *International Journal of Bilingual Education and Bilingualism*, *12*(3), 261–71. http://dx.doi.org/10.1080/13670050903003751

Cuthberson, R. (2012, June 12). Calgary school board reverses decision on bus fees: A flat rate will now apply to ride bus system. *Calgary Herald.* Retrieved from http://www.calgaryherald.com/news/Calgary+school+board+reverses+decision+fees/6741139/story.html

Cyre, J., & Fyre, D. (2004). Rankings as a catalyst: Improving student performance. *Education Canada*, *44*(3), 34–6.

Daleney, C.F. (1994). *The liberalism-communitarian debate.* Lanham, MD: Rowman and Littlefield.

Davidson, T. (2011, July 7). Public schools prayer sessions criticized. *Toronto Sun.* Retrieved from http://www.torontosun.com/2011/07/07/public-school-prayer-sessions-criticized

Davies, S., & Aurini, J. (2003). Homeschooling and Canadian educational politics: Rights, pluralism and pedagogical individualism. *Evaluation and Research in Education*, *17*(2-3), 63–73. http://dx.doi.org/10.1080/09500790308668292

Davies, S., & Aurini, J. (2008). School choice as concerted cultivation: The case of Canada. In M. Forsey, S. Davies, & G. Walford (Eds.), *The globalisation of school choice?* (pp. 55–72). Oxford, England: Symposium Books.

Davies, S., & Aurini, J. (2011). Exploring school choice in Canada. Who choses what and why? *Canadian Public Policy*, *37*(4), 459–77. http://dx.doi.org/10.3138/cpp.37.4.459

Department for Education & Gove, M. (2011, June 20). Michael Gove's speech to the Policy Exchange on free schools. Retrieved from https://www.gov.uk/

government/speeches/michael-goves-speech-to-the-policy-exchange-on-free-schools

Department for Education, Gov.UK. (1997). *Excellence in schools*. London, England: Stationery Office.

Dewey, J. (1966). *Democracy and education. An introduction to the philosophy of education*. New York, NY: Free Press. (Original work published 1916)

Doucet, C. (2002). *Edgerton Ryerson, 1803–1882*. Asc archives + special collections. Retrieved from http://library.ryerson.ca/asc/archives/ryerson-history/ryerson-bio/

Doyle, G. (2012). *French immersion in Canada*. Retrieved from http://hrsbstaff.ednet.ns.ca/gdoyle1/secondarypage/french_immersion_in_canada.htm

Dragnea, C., & Erling, S. (2008). *The effectiveness of Africentric (black-focused) schools in closing student success and achievement gaps: A review of the literature*. Etobicoke, ON: Toronto District School Board.

Drucker, P. (1993). *Post-capitalist society*. New York, NY: Harper Business.

Duncan, G. & Murname, R. (Eds.). (2011). *Whither opportunity? Rising inequality, schools and children's life chances*. New York, NY: Russell Sage Foundations and Spencer Foundation.

Economic Council of Canada. (1992). *A lot to learn: Education and training in Canada*. Ottawa, ON: Supply and Services Canada. Retrieved from https://www.econbiz.de/Record/a-lot-to-learn-education-and-training-in-canada-a-statement-by-the-economic-council-of-canada/10000840559

Edmonton Logos Society. (2015). Welcome to the website for the Edmonton Logos Society! Retrieved from http://www.christianprogram.ca/

Edmonton Public School Board. (1974). *Alternatives in education: Report presented to the Edmonton Committee, Edmonton Public School Board by the administration*. Edmonton, AB: Author.

Edmonton Public School Board. (2012). Mission, vision, priorities and philosophy. Retrieved from http://ww2.epsb.ca/about/mission.shtml

Egea-Kuehne, D. (2012). Provoking curriculum studies in multicultural societies. In N. Ng-A-Fook & J. Rottmann (Eds.), *Reconsidering historical, present, and future perspectives* (pp. 137–48). New York, NY: Palgrave Macmillan.

Ekwa-Ekoko, I. (2008). *Africentric schools within a multicultural context: Exploring different attitudes towards TDSB proposal with the black community* (Theses and dissertations, Paper 82). Ryerson University. Retrieved from http://digital.library.ryerson.ca/dissertations/82

Etzioni, A. (1993). *The spirit of community*. New York, NY: Crown.

Fallon, G., & Paquette, J. (2008). Devolution, choice and accountability in the provision of public education in British Columbia: A critical analysis of the School Amendment Act of 2002 (Bill 34). *Canadian Journal of Educational*

Administration and Policy, 75, 1–36. Retrieved from http://www.umanitoba.ca/publications/cjeap/pdf_files/fallonpaquette.pdf

Feinberg, W. (1998). *Common schools/uncommon identities: National unity and cultural difference.* New Haven, CT: Yale University Press.

Fontaine, T. (2010). *Broken circle: The dark legacy of Indian residential schools: A memoir.* Victoria, BC: Heritage House.

Forsey, M., Davies, S., & Walford, G. (2008). The globalisation of school choice? An introduction to key issues and concerns. In M. Forsey, S. Davies, & G. Walford (Eds.), *The globalisation of school choice* (pp. 9–26). Oxford, England: Symposium.

Fried, R. (1998). Parent anxiety and school reform: When interests collide, whose needs come first? *Phi Delta Kappan, 80,* 264–71. Retrieved from http://www.jstor.org/stable/20439424

Friedman, M. (1962). *Capitalism and freedom.* Chicago, IL: University of Chicago Press.

Friesen, S., Clifford, P., Jacobsen, M., & Jardine, D. (2005). Teaching and learning in a knowledge society. Retrieved from the Galileo Foundation website: http://www.galileo.org/research.html

Friesen, S., Clifford, P., & Lock, J. (2004). *Coming to teaching in the 21st century.* Retrieved from the Galileo Foundation website: http://www.galileo.org/research/publications/ctt.pdf

Friesen, S., & Jardine, D. (2009). *21st century learning and learners. Report prepared for the Western and Northern Canadian Curriculum Protocol.* Calgary, AB: Galileo Educational Network.

Fullan, M. (2013). *Great to excellent: Launching the next stage of Ontario's education agenda.* Retrieved from http://www.edu.gov.on.ca/eng/document/reports/FullanReport_EN_07.pdf

Galston, W. (1999). Expressive liberty, moral pluralism, political pluralism: Three sources of liberal theory. *William and Mary Law review, 40*(3), 869–907. Retrieved from http://scholarship.law.wm.edu/wmlr/vol40/iss3/9

Galston, W. (2002). *Liberal pluralism: the implications of value pluralism for political theory and practice.* Cambridge: Cambridge University Press. http://dx.doi.org/10.1017/CBO9780511613579

Gaskell, J. (2001). The public in public schools: A school board debate. *Canadian Journal of Education, 26*(1), 19–36. http://dx.doi.org/10.2307/1602143

Gaskell, J. (2002a). Creating school choice: The politics of curriculum, equity and teachers' work. *Canadian Public Policy/Analyse de Politiques, 28*(1), 39–50. http://dx.doi.org/10.2307/3552158

Gaskell, J. (2002b). School choice and educational leadership: Rethinking the future of public schooling. In K. Leithwood & P. Hallinger (Eds.), *Second*

International Handbook of Educational Leadership and Administration (pp. 915–55). Dordrecht, Netherlands: Kluwer Academic Publishers. http://dx.doi .org/10.1007/978-94-010-0375-9_31

Gaskell, J., & Levin, B. (2012). *Making a difference in urban schools: Ideas, politics, and pedagogy.* Toronto: University of Toronto Press.

Gereluk, D. (2006). *Education and community.* New York, NY: Continuum.

Gereluk, D. (2008). *Symbolic clothing in schools: What should be worn and why.* New York, NY: Continuum.

Gereluk, D. (2011). Good intentions gone awry: Limiting toleration and diversity through Bill 44. Canadian Issue (Special Issue of the *Comparative and International Studies Society*), 75–9. Retrieved from http://www.acs-aec.ca/pdf/ pubs/toc/CanadianIssues_d_toc.pdf

Gereluk, D., & Scott, D. (2014). Citizenship education and the construction of identity in Canada. In J.E. Petrovic & A.M. Kuntz (Eds.), *Citizenship education around the world: Local contexts and global possibilities* (pp. 128–49). New York, NY: Routledge University Press.

Gewirtz, S., Ball, S., & Bowe, R. (1995). *Markets, choice and equity in education.* Buckingham, England: Open University Press.

Gidney, R.D. (1999). *From hope to Harris: The reshaping of Ontario's schools.* Toronto, ON: University of Toronto Press.

Gillespie, K. (2007, July 24). John Tory puts faith in school religion. *The Star.* Retrieved from http://www.thestar.com/news/ontario/2007/07/24/john_ tory_puts_faith_in_school_religion.html

Glenn, C. (2015). Balancing the interests of the state and citizens. *Journal of School Choice: International Research and Reform, 9*(1), 139–51. http://dx.doi.org /10.1080/15582159.2015.1000776

Godfrey, T. (2011a, July 5). Muslim group wants prayers in public schools stopped. *Toronto Sun.* Retrieved from http://www.torontosun.com/2011/07/ 05/muslim-group-wants-prayer-in-public-school-stopped

Godfrey, T. (2011b, August 8). Parents fear imams turn kids into radicals. *Toronto Sun.* Retrieved from http://www.edmontonsun.com/2011/08/08/ parents-fear-imams-turn-kids-into-radicals

Godwin, K., & Kemerer, F. (2002). *School choice tradeoffs: Liberty, equity, and diversity.* Austin, TX: University of Texas Press.

Goldthorpe, J., & Jackson, M. (2008). Education-based meritocracy: The barriers to its realization. In A. Lareau & D. Conley (Eds.), *Social class: How does it work?* (pp. 93–117). New York, NY: Russell Sage Foundation.

Goodenow, R. (1988). Schooling, identity and denomination: The American experience. In W. Tulasiewicz & C. Brock (Eds.), *Christianity and educational provisions and international perspective* (pp. 93–117). London, England: Routledge.

Gordon, M., & Zinga, D. (2012). "Fear of stigmatization": Black Canadian youths' reactions to the implementation of a black-focused school in Toronto. *Canadian Journal of Educational Administration and Policy, 131,* 1–37. Retrieved from https://www.umanitoba.ca/publications/cjeap/pdf_files/gordon_zinga.pdf

Government of Alberta. (2011). *Action on research and innovation. The future of charter schools in Alberta.* Retrieved from http://education.alberta.ca/media/6735500/thefutureofcharterschoolsinalberta.pdf

Government of Alberta. (2012). *Charter schools regulation.* Retrieved from http://www.qp.alberta.ca/documents/Regs/2002_212.pdf

Government of Canada. (1965). *Preliminary report of the royal commission on bilingualism and biculturalism.* Ottawa, ON: Queen's Printer.

Government of Canada. (1967). *Book I: The official languages.* Ottawa, ON: Queen's Printer.

Government of Canada (1968). *Statement on the introduction of the Official Language Bill, October 17, 1968.* Retrieved from Library Archives of Canada https://www.collectionscanada.gc.ca/primeministers/h4-4066-e.html

Government of Canada. (1969a). *Report of the royal commission on bilingualism and biculturalism: Book III: The world of work.* Ottawa, ON: Queen's Printer.

Government of Canada. (1969b). *Report of the royal commission on bilingualism and biculturalism: Book IV: The cultural contribution of the other ethnic groups.* Ottawa, ON: Queen's Printer.

Government of Canada. (2010). *Memorandum of understanding for First Nations education in Alberta.* Retrieved from https://education.alberta.ca/media/1227766/mou%20for%20first%20nations%20education%20in%20alberta.pdf?

Government of Canada. (2014a). *The Canadian charter of rights and freedoms.* Retrieved from http://publications.gc.ca/collections/Collection/CH37-4-3-2002E.pdf

Government of Canada. (2014b). *Canadian multiculturalism act.* Retrieved from http://laws-lois.justice.gc.ca/eng/acts/C-18.7/page-1.html

Government of Canada. (2014c). *Constitution act, 1867.* Retrieved from http://laws.justice.gc.ca/eng/Const/page-1.html

Government of Canada, Human Resource Development Canada. (2002). *Knowledge matters: Skills and learning for Canadians.* Ottawa, ON: Author.

Government of Canada, Industry Canada. (2002). *Achieving excellence: Investing in people, knowledge and opportunity.* Ottawa, ON: Author.

Government of Ontario. (2012). *An act to amend the education act with respect to bullying and other matters.* Retrieved from http://ontla.on.ca/web/bills/bills_detail.do?locale=en&BillID=2549

Guillemette, Y. (2007). *Breaking down monopolies: Expanding choice and competition in education.* Toronto, ON: C.D. Howe Institute.

Gutmann, A. (1987). *Democratic education*. Princeton, NJ: Princeton University Press.

Gutmann, A. (1994). Introduction. In A. Gutman (Ed.), *Multiculturalism: Examining the politics of recognition* (pp. 3–24). Princeton, NJ: Princeton University Press.

Harrison, T., & Kachur, J. (1999). *Contested classrooms: Education, globalization and democracy in Alberta*. Edmonton, AB: University of Alberta Press.

Harvey, D. (2009). *A brief history of neoliberalism*. Oxford, England: Oxford University Press.

Hatcher, R. (1998). Class differentiation in education: Rational choices? *British Journal of Education, 19*, 5–24. http://dx.doi.org/10.1080/0142569980190101

Hepburn, C. (Ed.). (2001). *Can the market save our schools?* Vancouver, BC: The Fraser Institute.

Hess, F. (2009). A market for knowledge? In G. Sykes, B. Schneider, & D. Plank (Eds.), *Handbook of education policy research* (pp. 502–512). New York, NY: Routledge.

Hewitt, V.M. (2001). Examining the Reggio Emilia approach to early childhood education. *Early Childhood Education Journal, 29*(2), 95–100. http://dx.doi.org/10.1023/A:1012520828095

Hill, P. (2010). *Learning as we go: Why school choice is worth the wait*. Stanford, CA: Hoover Institute Press.

Hill, T., & Guin, K. (2003). Baselines for assessment for choice programs. *Education Policy Analysis Archives, 11*(39), 1–31. http://dx.doi.org/10.14507/epaa.v11n39.2003

Holmes, M. (1998). *The reformation of Canada's schools: Breaking barriers to parental choice*. Montreal, QC: McGill-Queens University Press.

Holmes, M. (2008). An update on school choice in Canada. *Journal of School Choice, 2*(2), 199–205. http://dx.doi.org/10.1080/15582150802138229

Employment and Social Development Canada. (2014). Standards and equity – Main page. Labour program. Retrieved from http://www.labour.gc.ca/eng/standards_equity/index.shtml

Hyslop, K. (2011a, September 14). Amidst the big city, an Aboriginal public school? *The Tyee*. Retrieved from http://thetyee.ca/News/2011/09/14/Vancouver-Aboriginal-School-Proposal/

Hyslop, K. (2011b, September 6). How Chief Atahm Elementary School became a success story. *The Tyee*. Retrieved from http://thetyee.ca/News/2011/09/06/Chief-Atahm-Elementary-School/

James, C.E., & Brathwaite, K.S. (1996). The education of African Canadians: Issues, contexts, and expectations. In K.S. Brathwaite & C.E. James (Eds.), *Educating African Canadians* (pp. 13–31). Toronto, ON: James Lorimer.

Johnson, D. (2013). *Identifying Alberta's best schools* (C.D. Howe Institute E-Brief 164). Retrieved from http://www.cdhowe.org/pdf/e-brief_164.pdf

Kalambouka, A., Farrell, P., Dyson, A., & Kaplan, I. (2007). The impact of placing pupils with special educational needs in mainstream schools on the achievement of their peers. *Educational Research, 49*(4), 365–382. http://dx.doi.org/10.1080/00131880701717222

Katz, J. (2012). *Teaching to diversity: The three-block model of universal design for learning.* Winnipeg, Manitoba: Portage & Main Press.

Kennedy, M. (2014, May 3). Shawn Atleo resigns as Assembly of First Nations national chief. *Postmedia News.* Retrieved from http://o.canada.com/news/shawn-atleo-resigning-as-assembly-of-first-nations-national-chief

Kunzman, R. (2010). Homeschooling and religious fundamentalism. *International Electronic Journal of Elementary Education, 3*(1), 16–28. Retrieved from https://www.pegem.net/dosyalar/dokuman/138518-20140104174110-3.pdf

Kunzman, R. (2012). Education, schooling and children's rights: The complexity of homeschooling. *Educational Theory, 62*(1), 75–89. http://dx.doi.org/10.1111/j.1741-5446.2011.00436.x

Kymlicka, W. (1998). *Finding our way: Rethinking ethnocultural relations in Canada.* Toronto, ON: Oxford University Press.

Kymlicka, W. (2007). *Multicultural odysseys: Navigating the new international politics of diversity.* Oxford, England: Oxford University Press.

Kymlicka, W. (2008). *The three lives of multiculturalism.* Paper presented at the UBC-Laurier Institution Multiculturalism Lecture Series, Vancouver, British Columbia. Retrieved from https://www.academia.edu/2397536/The_Three_Lives_of_Multiculturalism_2008_

Lamont, J., & Favor, C. (2013). Distributive justice. *Stanford Encyclopedia of Philosophy.* Retrieved from http://plato.stanford.edu/entries/justice-distributive/#Difference

Lareau, A. (2002). Invisible inequality: Social class and childrearing in black families and white families. *American Sociological Review, 67*(5), 747–76. http://dx.doi.org/10.2307/3088916

Lareau, A., & Weininger, E. (2008). Time, work and family life: Reconceptualising gendered time patterns through the case of children's organized activities. *Sociological Forum, 23*(3), 419–54. http://dx.doi.org/10.1111/j.1573-7861.2008.00085.x

Lawton, S. (2001). *Educational finance and school choice in the United States and Canada (Occasional paper no. 17).* New York, NY: National Center for the Study of Privatization in Education.

Lawton, S., Freedman, S., & Robertson, H.J. (1995). *Busting bureaucracy to reclaim our schools.* Montreal, QC: Institute for Research on Public Policy.

Lindholm-Leary, K. (2001). *Dual language education.* Clevedon, England: Multilingual Matters.

Lingard, B., & Christie, P. (2003). Leading theory: Bourdieu and the field of educational leadership. An introduction and overview to this special issue. *International Journal of Leadership in Education: Theory and Practice, 6*(4), 317–33. http://dx.doi.org/10.1080/1360312032000150724

Lubienski, C. (2003). Innovation in education markets: Theory and evidence on the impact of competition and choice in charter schools. *American Educational Research Journal, 40*(2), 395–443. http://dx.doi.org/10.3102/00028312040002395

Lubienski, C. (2012). Education innovation and diversification in school choice plans. In G. Miron, K. Welner, P. Hinchey, & W. Mathis (Eds.), *Exploring the school choice universe: Evidence and recommendations* (pp. 147–65). Charlotte, NC: Information Age Publishing.

Lucey, H., & Reay, D. (2002). Carrying the beacon of excellence: Social class differentiation and anxiety at the time of transition. *Journal of Education Policy, 17*(3), 321–36. http://dx.doi.org/10.1080/02680930210127586

Lukaszuk, T. (2012). *Minor regulation changes for coveted charter schools.* Retrieved from http://www.cbc.ca/news/canada/calgary/minor-regulation-changes-made-for-coveted-charter-schools-1.1274695

Luke, C. (2003, April). Home schooling: Learning from dissent. *Canadian Journal of Educational Administration and Policy, 2003*(25). Retrieved from https://www.umanitoba.ca/publications/cjeap/articles/caluke.html

MacIntyre, A. (1984). *After virtue* (2nd ed.). Notre Dame, IN: University of Notre Dame Press.

Macnab, J. (2010). *Investigation on the longitudinal effects of immersion and bilingual programs on first language development.* Edmonton, AB: Confucius Institute in Edmonton.

Madvor, M. (1995). *Aboriginal students. First Nations education in Canada: The circle unfolds.* Vancouver, BC: UBC Press.

Maguire, P. (2006). *Choice in urban school systems: The Edmonton experience.* Kelowna, BC: Society for the Advancement of Excellence in Education.

Mahe v. Alberta, [1990] 1 SCR, 342.

Manley-Casimir, C. M. (Ed). (1982). *Family choice in schooling: Issues and dilemmas.* Lexington, MA: Lexington Books.

Maxwell, B., Waddington, D., McDonough, K., Cormier, A., & Schwimmer, M. (2012). Interculturalism, multiculturalism, and the state funding of conservative religious schools. *Educational Theory, 62*(4), 427–47. http://dx.doi.org/10.1111/j.1741-5446.2012.00455.x

McAndrew, M. (2001). *Immigration et diversité l'école: le débat québécois dans une perspective comparative.* [Immigration and diversity school: Quebec debate in comparative perspective] Montreal, QC: Presses de l'Université de Montréal.

McLaughlin, T. (2005). School choice and public education in a liberal democratic society. *American Journal of Education, 111*(4), 442–463. http://dx.doi.org/10.1086/432026

Mendelson, M. (2008). *Improving education on reserves: A First Nations education authority act.* Ottawa, ON: Caledon Institute of Public Policy. Retrieved from http://www.caledoninst.org/publications/pdf/684eng.pdf

Merrifield, J. (2008). The twelve policy approaches to increased school choice. *Journal of School Choice, 2*(1), 4–19. http://dx.doi.org/10.1080/15582150802007267

Merry, M. (2012). Equality, self-respect and voluntary separation. *Critical Review of International Social and Political Philosophy, 15*(1), 79–100. http://dx.doi.org/10.1080/13698230.2010.528239

Merry, M., & Karsten, S. (2010). Restricted liberty, parental choice and home-schooling. *Journal of Philosophy of Education, 44*(4), 497–514. Retrieved from http://dare.uva.nl/personal/record/330488. http://dx.doi.org/10.1111/j.1467-9752.2010.00770.x

Mi'kmaw Kina'matnewey. (2014). *An A+ for Mi'kmaq education.* Retrieved from http://kinu.ca/success/mikmaq-education

Miller, R. (1986). Should there be religious alternative schools within the public school system? *Canadian Journal of Education, 11*(3), 278–92. http://dx.doi.org/10.2307/1494433

Miron, G., & Welner, K. (2012). Introduction. In G. Miron, K. Welner, P. Hinchey, & W. Mathis (Eds.), *Exploring the school choice universe: Evidence and recommendations* (pp. 1–16). Charlotte, NC: Information Age Publishing.

Molnar, A. (1996). *Giving kids the business: The commercialization of America's schools.* Boulder, CO: Westview Press.

Murnaghan, C. (2009). *The educative practices of public alternative educators around student choice and student-directed learning in the Ontario context* (Unpublished master's thesis). University of Toronto, Ontario, Canada.

National Commission on Excellence in Education. (1983). *A nation at risk: The imperative for educational reform.* Washington, DC: U.S. Department of Education.

National Panel on First Nation Elementary and Secondary Education for Students on Reserve. (2011). *Nurturing the learning spirit of First Nations students. The Report of the National Panel on First Nation Elementary and Secondary Education for Students on Reserve.* Retrieved from https://www.aadnc-aandc.gc.ca/eng/1373075023560/1373075345812

New Brunswick Department of Education. (2010). *NB3–21C: Creating a 21st century learning model of public education: Three-year plan 2010–2013.* Retrieved from https://roynorris.wikispaces.com/file/view/NB3-21C_consultation_document_2nd_edition.pdf/180173773/NB3-21C_consultation_document_2nd_edition.pdf

No Child Left Behind Act of 2001, Pub. L. No. 107-110, § 115, Stat. 1425 (2002).

Norris, T. (2011). *Consuming schools: Commercialism and the end of politics.* Toronto, ON: University of Toronto Press.

Nunavut struggles to offer Inuit-language education. (2011, June 28). *CBC News.* Retrieved from http://www.cbc.ca/news/canada/north/nunavut-struggles-to-offer-inuit-language-education-1.1088863

Office of the Commissioner of Official Languages. (2015). *Understanding your language rights.* Retrieved from http://www.officiallanguages.gc.ca/en/language_rights/act

Ontario Ministry of Education. (1968). *Living and learning: The report of the provincial committee on aims and objectives of education in the schools of Ontario.* Retrieved from http://www.connexions.org/CxLibrary/Docs/CX5636-HallDennis.htm

Ontario Ministry of Education. (2011). *Ontario schools kindergarten to grade 12: Policy and program requirements.* Retrieved from http://edu.gov.on.ca/eng/document/policy/os/ONSchools.pdf

Ontario Ministry of Education. (2014). *Ontario achieving excellence: A renewed vision for education in Ontario.* Retrieved from http://www.edu.gov.on.ca/eng/

Ouchi, W. (with Segal, L). (2003). *Making schools work: A revolutionary plan to get your children the education they need.* New York, NY: Simon & Schuster.

Palliser Regional Schools. (2015). *Faith-based alternative programs.* Retrieved from http://www.pallisersd.ab.ca/schools/faith-based-alternative-programs.

Palmater, P. (2014, May 16). Harper's assimilation agenda just collided with First Nation resistance—and lost. *Rabble.ca.* Retrieved from http://rabble.ca/blogs/bloggers/pamela-palmater/2014/05/harpers-assimilation-agenda-just-collided-first-nations-resis

Parliament of Canada. (2014). *Bill C-33: First Nations control of First Nations education.* Retrieved from http://www.parl.gc.ca/HousePublications/Publication.aspx?Language=E&Mode=1&DocId=6532106

Partnership for 21st Century Skills. (n.d.). *Framework for 21st century learning.* Retrieved from http://www.p21.org/our-work/p21-framework

Petition calls for back to the basics math in Alberta schools. (2014, March 11). *CBC News.* Retrieved from http://www.cbc.ca/news/canada/edmonton/petition-calls-for-back-to-basics-math-in-alberta-schools-1.2569045

Power, S. (2004). Comments on "how not to be a hypocrite": School choice for the morally perplexed. *Theory and Research in Education, 2*(1), 23–9. http://dx.doi.org/10.1177/1477878504040575

Power, S., Edwards, T., Whitty, G., & Wigfall, V. (2003). *Education and middle class.* Buckingham, England: Open University Press.

Pring, R. (2008). The common school. In M. Halstead & G. Haydon (Eds.), *The common school and the comprehensive ideal: A defence by Richard Pring with complementary essays* (pp. 1–19). Sussex, England: Wiley-Blackwell. http://dx.doi.org/10.1002/9781444307313.ch1

Quebec Ministry of Education. (2001). *Quebec education program: Preschool education and Elementary Education.* Retrieved from http://www1.mels.gouv.qc.ca/sections/programmeFormation/primaire/pdf/educprg2001/educprg2001.pdf

Quebec Ministry of Education. (2004). *Quebec education program: Secondary school education, cycle one.* Retrieved from http://www1.mels.gouv.qc.ca/sections/programmeFormation/secondaire1/pdf/qepsecfirstcycle.pdf

R. v. Jones, [1986] 2 S.C.R. 284.

Ranson, S. (1993). Markets or democracy for education. *British Journal of Educational Studies, 41*(4), 333–52. http://dx.doi.org/10.1080/00071005.1993.9973971

Ravitch, D. (2010). *The death and life of the great American school system: How testing and choice are undermining education.* New York, NY: Basic Books.

Rawls, J. (1985). Justice as fairness: political not metaphysical. *Philosophy & Public Affairs, 14*(3), 223–51. Retrieved from http://www.jstor.org/stable/2265349

Rawls, J. (1993). *Political liberalism.* New York, NY: Columbia University Press.

Rawls, J. (1999). *A theory of justice* (rev. ed.). Oxford, England: Oxford University Press.

Rawls, J. (2001). *Justice as fairness: A restatement.* E. Kelly (Ed.). Cambridge, MA: Harvard University Press.

Reay, D., & Ball, S. (2005). *Degrees of choice: Class, race, gender and higher education.* London, England: Trentham Books.

Regan, P. (2010). *Unsettling the settler within: Indian residential schools, truth telling, and reconciliation in Canada.* Vancouver, BC: UBC Press.

Reich, R. (2002a). The civil perils of homeschooling. *Educational Leadership, 59*(7), 56–9.

Reich, R. (2002b). *Bridging liberalism and multiculturalism in American education.* Chicago, London: University of Chicago Press.

Reich, R. (2005). Why homeschooling should be regulated. In B. Cooper (Ed.), *Homeschooling in full view: A reader* (pp. 109–120). Greenwich, CT: Information Age Publishing.

Reich, R. (2007). How and why to support common schooling and educational choice at the same time. *Journal of Philosophy of Education, 41*(4), 709–25. http://dx.doi.org/10.1111/j.1467-9752.2007.00578.x

Reich, R. (2008). Common schooling and educational choice as a response to pluralism. In W. Feinberg & C. Lubienski (Eds.), *School choice policies and outcomes: Empirical and philosophical perspectives* (pp. 21–40). New York, NY: SUNY Press.

Richardson, G. (2002). *The death of the good Canadian: Teachers, national identities, and the social studies curriculum.* New York, NY: Peter Lang.

Riffel, T., Levin, B., & Young, J. (1996). Diversity in Canadian education. *Journal of Education Policy, 11*(1), 113–23. http://dx.doi.org/10.1080/0268093960110106

Ritchie, S. (2010). *Innovations in action: An examination of charter schools in Alberta. The West in Canada Research Series.* Calgary, AB: Canada West Foundation.

Ross, C.J. (2010). Fundamentalist challenges to core democratic values: Exit and homeschooling. *William and Mary Bill of Rights Journal, 18,* 991–1014. Retrieved from http://scholarship.law.wm.edu/cgi/viewcontent.cgi?article=1160&context=wmborj

Rothstein, H. (1999). *Alternative schools in British Columbia, 1960–1975* (Unpublished doctoral dissertation). University of British Columbia, Vancouver, Canada.

Royal Commission on Aboriginal Peoples. (1996). *Gathering strength* (Vol. 3). Ottawa, ON: Author.

Ryerson, D. (1847). *Report on a system of public elementary instruction for Upper Canada.* Montreal, QC: Lovell & Gibson. Retrieved from https://openlibrary .org/books/OL25490529M/Report_on_a_system_of_public_elementary_ instruction_for_Upper_Canada

Sandel, M. (1998). *Liberalism and the limits of justice* (2nd ed.). Cambridge, UK: Cambridge University Press. http://dx.doi.org/10.1017/CBO9780511810152

Sands, A. (2013, January 25). Edmonton public schools turn down proposal for Victoria high-school students to meet entrance requirements. *Edmonton Journal.* Retrieved from http://www.edmontonsun.com/2013/01/25/ edmonton-public-school-board-nixes-proposal-to-have-auditions-for-high-school-students-to-be-admitted-to-victoria-school-of-the-arts-in-edmonton

School Act, RSA 2000, c S-3, http://canlii.ca/t/528fl

Schwartz, D. (2013, November 4). First Nations education needs fresh ideas, leaders say. *CBC News.* Retrieved from http://www.cbc.ca/news/canada/ first-nations-education-needs-fresh-ideas-leaders-say-1.2255180

Sheenan, N. (1994). The origins and development of schooling in Canada. In R. O'Reilly & S. Sikora (Eds.), *Becoming a Canadian teacher* (pp. 43–54). Calgary, AB: University of Calgary.

Schrag, F. (1998). Diversity, schooling and the liberal state. *Studies in Philosophy and Education, 17*(1), 29–46. http://dx.doi.org/10.1023/A:1005020602073

Slee, R. (2011). *The irregular school: Exclusion, schooling, and inclusive education.* London, England: Routledge.

Smith, J., Wohlstetter, P., Farrell, C., & Nayfack, M. (2011). Beyond ideological warfare: The maturation of research on charter schools. *Journal of School Choice: International Research and Reform, 5*(4), 444–507. http://dx.doi.org/10.1080/15582159.2011.624938

Statistics Canada. (2006). *Educational portrait of Canada, 2006 Census.* Retrieved from http://www12.statcan.ca/census-recensement/2006/as-sa/97-560/pdf/97-560-XIE2006001.pdf

Steering Group on Prosperity. (1992). *Inventing our future: An action plan for Canada's prosperity.* Ottawa, ON: Author.

Stein, J. (2007). Searching for equality. In J. Stein (Ed.), *Uneasy partners: Multiculturalism and rights in Canada* (pp. 1–22). Waterloo, ON: Wilfred Laurier University Press.

Steiner, R. (1985). *An introduction to Waldorf education (Revised by F. Amrine; E. Bowen-Wedgewood, Trans.).* Great Barrington, MA: Anthroposophic Press. (Original work published 1919).

Supreme Court of Canada. (2008). *The impact of the Supreme Court of Canada on bilingualism and biculturalism.* Retrieved from http://www.scc-csc.gc.ca/court-cour/judges-juges/spe-dis/bm-2008-02-06-eng.aspx

Swift, A. (2003). *How not to be a hypocrite: School choice for the morally perplexed parent.* New York, NY: Routledge.

T'selcéwtqen Clleqmél'ten. (2013). *Chief Atahm Elementary School.* Retrieved from http://www.chiefatahm.com

Talmud Torah Society. (2011). *Talmud Torah school.* Retrieved from http://www.talmudtorahsociety.com/about/faq/

Taylor, A. (2001a). "Fellow travelers" and "true believers": A case study of religion and politics in Alberta schools. *Journal of Education Policy, 16*(1), 15–37. http://dx.doi.org/10.1080/02680930010009804

Taylor, A. (2001b). *The politics of educational reform in Alberta.* Toronto, ON: University of Toronto Press.

Taylor, A., & Mackay, J. (2008). Three decades of choice in Edmonton schools. *Journal of Education Policy, 23*(5), 549–66. http://dx.doi.org/10.1080/02680930802192774

Taylor, A., & Woollard, L. (2003). The risky business of choosing a high school. *Journal of Education Policy, 18*(6), 617–35. http://dx.doi.org/10.1080/0268093032000145872

Taylor, C. (1985). *Philosophy and the human sciences: Philosophical papers 2.*
   Cambridge, UK: Cambridge University Press. http://dx.doi.org/10.1017/
   CBO9781139173490

Taylor, C. (1994). Politics of recognition. In A. Gutmann (Ed.), *Multiculturalism:
   Examining the politics of recognition* (pp. 25–49). Princeton, NJ: Princeton
   University Press.

Thiessen, E. (2001). *In defence of religious schools and colleges.* Montreal, QC:
   McGill-Queens University Press.

Thomas, W., & Collier, V. (2002). *A national study of school effectiveness for
   language minority students' long-term academic achievement.* Berkeley, CA: UC
   Berkeley Center for Research on Education, Diversity and Excellence.

Titley, B., & Miller, P. (1982). *Education in Canada: An interpretation.* Calgary, AB:
   Detselig Enterprises.

Tooley, J. (2000). *Reclaiming education.* London, England: Cassell.

Trans-Davies, N. (2014). Alberta discovery curriculum fails the kids. *The Globe
   and Mail.* Retrieved from http://www.theglobeandmail.com/news/national/
   education/alberta-education-reforms-ignore-kids-parents/article17390684/

Truth and Reconciliation Commission of Canada. (2012). *Truth and
   Reconciliation Commission of Canada: Interim report.* Retrieved from http://
   www.myrobust.com/websites/trcinstitution/File/Interim%20report%
   20English%20electronic.pdf

University of British Columbia, First Nations Studies Program. (2009). *Reserves.*
   Indigenous Foundations. Retrieved from http://indigenousfoundations.arts
   .ubc.ca/home/government-policy/reserves.html

Van Pelt, N. D. (2015). *Homeschooling in Canada: The current picture.* Vancouver:
   The Fraser Institute. Retrieved from https://www.fraserinstitute.org/sites/
   default/files/home-schooling-in-canada-2015-rev2.pdf

Vancouver francophone parents win Supreme Court of Canada ruling. (2015,
   April 24). *CBC News.* Retrieved from http://www.cbc.ca/news/canada/
   british-columbia/vancouver-francophone-parents-win-supreme-court-of-
   canada-ruling-1.3047309

Vaughan, M. (Ed.). (2006). *Summerhill and A. S. Neill.* New York, NY: Open
   University Press.

Wells, A. (1997). African-American students' view of school choice. In A.H.
   Halsey, H. Lauder, P. Brown, & A.S. Wells (Eds.), *Education, culture, economy
   and society* (pp. 422–38). Oxford, England: Oxford University Press.

Wente, M. (2014, June 28). The brave new world of 21st century learning.
   The Globe and Mail. Retrieved from http://www.theglobeandmail.com/
   globe-debate/the-brave-new-world-of-21st-century-learning/article19355298/

Whitty, G., Power, S., & Halpin, D. (1998). *Devolution and choice in education: The school, the state and the market.* Buckingham, England: Open University Press.

Wilson, D. (1970). The Ryerson years in Canada West. In J.D. Wilson, R.M. Stamp, & L.P. Audet (Eds.), *Canadian education: A history* (pp. 214–40). Scarborough, ON: Prentice-Hall.

Wilson, J. (1991). Does equality of opportunity make sense in education? *Journal of Philosophy of Education, 25*(1), 27–32. http://dx.doi.org/10.1111/j.1467-9752.1991.tb00246.x

Wilson, J. (2007). *Faith-based schools. CBC News.* Retrieved from http://www.cbc.ca/ontariovotes2007/features/features-faith.html

Wilson, T. (2012). Negotiating public and private: Philosophical frameworks for school choice. In G. Miron, K. Welner, P. Hinchey, & W. Mathis (Eds.), *Exploring the school choice universe* (pp. 17–38). Charlotte, NC: Information Age Publishing.

Wright, E.O. (2008). Logics of class analysis. In A. Lareau & D. Conley (Eds.), *Social class: How does it work?* (pp. 329–49). New York, NY: Russell Sage Foundation.

Wu, J., & Bilash, O. (2000, January). *Bilingual education in practice: A multifunctional model of minority language programs in Western Canada.* Paper presented at the Hawaii International Conference on Education, Honolulu, Hawaii.

Young, M. (1958). *The rise of meritocracy.* London, England: Thames and Hudson.

Yuen, J. (2011a, July 25). Muslim prayers in public schools protested. *Toronto Sun.* Retrieved from http://www.edmontonsun.com/2011/07/25/muslim-prayers-in-public-schools-protested

Yuen, J. (2011b, July 7). Protest planned over prayer sessions in Toronto. *Toronto Sun.* Retrieved from http://www.torontosun.com/2011/07/18/protest-planned-over-prayer-sessions-in-toronto-school

Yuracko, K.A. (2008). Education off the grid: Constitutional constraints on homeschooling. *California Law Review, 96*(1), 123–84. Retrieved from http://scholarship.law.berkeley.edu/cgi/viewcontent.cgi?article=1187&context=californialawreview

Zine, J. (2000). Redefining resistance: Towards an Islamic subculture in schools. *Race, Ethnicity and Education, 3*(3), 293–316. http://dx.doi.org/10.1080/713693042

Zylberberg v. Sudbury Board of Education, [1988] CanLII 189 (ON CA).

Index

Aboriginal education: about, 33, 35–43, 47–8; accommodations for diversity, 65; achievement disparities, 40–1, 118; Alberta schools, 40–2, 89, 106; band-operated schools, 38; Bill C–33 (control of education), 118–20; control by Aboriginal peoples, 10, 19, 32–3, 36–8, 41–2, 47–8, 115, 120–1; funding disparities, 38, 42, 47, 118–20; goals of, 38–40, 41–3; government/First Nations agreements, 41–2; historical background, 9, 35–8, 42, 48; Inuit, 35, 37, 39, 47, 120–1; language immersion programs, 39–40; liberal multiculturalism, 118–21; Mi'kmaq students, 39, 41, 121; as national minority group, 32–3, 116–17; official languages in territories, 39, 47; off-reserve schools, 38, 41–2; on-reserve schools, 38, 39–40, 41–2, 47, 118–20; recommended ethical principles, 115, 137–9; statistics, 38, 40, 118; traditional culture, 9, 33, 35, 37–40, 41–2, 48

academies. *See* alternative schools (programs); elite specialist schools (sports or arts); faith-based schools; heritage-language schools (programs)

accommodations for diversity: about, 4, 55–6, 68–9; anti-bullying legislation, 59; authentic recognition of diversity, 65–6; balance between individual rights and pluralism, 54–5, 57; Charter rights, 54–6, 68–9; classroom practices, 64–6; exit rights, 121–2; minority groups, 53–8; multiculturalism principles, 53–4; neoliberal reforms, 135; Quebec's interculturalism, 10, 51, 66–9; religious minority groups, 55–7, 60–1; tolerance and understanding, 54, 64–5; voluntary subcultures, 56

Achieving Excellence (Canada), 76–7

Adams Lake Reserve, 39–40

Adler v. Ontario, 60–1

Africentric schools (programs), 64, 114, 124–5, 138

Alberta: Aboriginal education, 40–2; alternative schools, 61, 75, 90, 103–4; anglophone, francophone, and French immersion, 45–6, 47(t); balance of individual *vs.*

group rights, 59–60, 68; Catholic and Protestant schools, 34–5, 62(t), 125; on continuum of school choice, 79; evaluation, 77, 87, 88; faith-based schools, 61, 62(t), 125–6; francophone separate schools, 46; gifted and talented students (GATE), 103–4; heritage-language schools, 63–4, 65(t); homeschooling, 13n4, 80(t), 82–3, 130; independent/private schools, 80(t), 85, 86(t), 87, 88; neoliberal-inspired reforms, 77, 85–8, 134–5; new provincial framework, 77–8; open enrolment, 80(t), 90, 92; parental control and controversial issues, 59–60; parent-based school councils, 87, 134–5; research on, 6, 98–100; second-language immersion programs, 64. *See also* charter schools, Alberta
Alberta, Mahe v., 46
Almadina Language Charter Academy, Calgary, 61, 89, 106
Alpha Alternative School, Toronto, 75
alternative schooling reforms. *See* history of education policy; school choice
alternative schools (programs): about, 12, 89–93, 109–11, 131; admission, 90, 91, 103–4, 106; Africentric schools, 64, 114, 124–5, 138; change from independent/private schools to, 75, 85, 90; charter school models, 88; costs, 90, 92, 107–8; critique of, 91–2, 93, 107, 131; with different philosophical orientation, 111, 131, 138–9; for disadvantaged students, 75, 93,

102, 124; equality of opportunity, 25, 102, 108; gifted education, 102, 103–4; goals of, 90–1; hierarchy of disciplines, 11, 107; historical background, 74–5, 90, 100–1; homogenous student populations *vs.* exposure to diversity, 92; liberal multiculturalism, 124–5; location of schools, 12, 29, 104–5, 106, 111; as magnets for middle-class students, 102, 106; multiculturalism principles, 53–4; open enrolment, 90–1, 92; recommended ethical principles, 131, 137–9; religious focus, 61; science programs, 102, 105; and social class, 102, 108; uniforms, 108–9. *See also* faith-based schools; French immersion schools (programs); homeschooling; independent/private schools
American Sign Language, 65(t), 132
Amish schools, 12
Amiskwaciy Academy, Edmonton, 40
anglophones. *See* English language and anglophones
anti-bullying legislation, 59
Arabic language, 65(t)
arts schools. *See* elite specialist schools (sports or arts)
Assembly of First Nations, 37–8, 39, 42, 118, 119
Atleo, Shawn, 119
at-risk students. *See* disadvantaged and marginalized students
attendance requirements, 13n5
Aurini, J., 82

Ball, D., 104–5, 107
Ball, S., 26
Ben-Porath, S., 98, 122, 127

Bilash, O., 123

bilingualism. *See* official languages

bisexual students. *See* LGBT students

Black students, 124–5. *See also* Africentric schools (programs)

Bouchard-Taylor report, 66, 69

boundaries, open. *See* open enrolment (intra-district)

Bourdieu, Pierre, 97

Boyle Street Education Centre, Edmonton, 89, 106, 136

Brighouse, H., 22, 29

British Columbia: Aboriginal education, 39–41; alternative schools, 61, 74–5, 90–1; anglophone, francophone, and French immersion, 45–6, 47(t); faith-based schools, 61, 62(t), 125–6; heritage-language programs, 64, 65(t); historical background, 74–5; homeschooling, 80(t), 81; independent/private schools, 80(t), 83, 85, 86(t); new provincial framework, 77–8; open enrolment, 80(t), 90; research by think tanks, 6n2; unschooling approach, 79, 81

British North America Act. *See* Constitution Act (1867)

bullying, 59

Calgary, Alberta: alternative schools, 61, 75, 102; charter schools, 61, 89, 106; gifted student (GATE) program, 103–4; historical background, 75; middle-class anxiety, 102

Canada West Foundation, 6, 77

Canadian Charter of Rights and Freedoms (1982): about, 10, 44, 69; accommodations for diversity, 54–6, 59, 68–9; anglophone rights, 44, 49; balance of individual *vs.* group rights, 68; control of minority language programs, 46; equality rights and equal protection under the law, 52; francophone rights outside Quebec, 8, 44, 46, 49; and French immersion, 49; historical background, 47; multicultural heritage under, 52; protection against religious discrimination, 60–1, 130

Canadian Multiculturalism Act (1988), 10, 53–5, 59, 63

Capitalism and Freedom (Friedman), 26–7

Caribbean Canadian students, 124–5. *See also* Africentric schools (programs)

Carson, T., 73

Catholics: accommodations for diversity, 57–9; enrolment statistics, 34, 62(t); faith-based schools, 62(t), 125–6; historical background, 33–5, 60–1; independent/private schools, 12; rights under Constitution Act, 33–5, 48, 60, 125

C.D. Howe Institute, 6, 77

Charter. *See* Canadian Charter of Rights and Freedoms (1982)

charter schools, Alberta: about, 12, 85–9, 92–3, 106; Aboriginal students, 40, 89, 106; admission, 12, 106–7; American charter schools, 136; costs and funding, 12, 87, 106–7, 108; critique of, 88–9, 93, 106–7; disadvantaged students, 89, 93, 106, 136; evaluation and testing, 87, 88; examples of, 40, 89, 106, 136; government regulation,

87–8; historical background, 77, 85–7, 134–5; neoliberal-inspired reforms, 85–7, 93; non-denominational, 12, 87, 106; research by, 89; research on, 88, 107, 136; and social class, 108, 136; statistics, 7, 87–8; teachers, 12, 87; transportation, 108; uniforms, 108–9

Chief Atahm Elementary School, British Columbia, 39–40

Christian schools (programs): accommodations for diversity, 57; alternative schools, 61; Christian values, 101; faith-based schools, 60–1, 62(t), 129–31; independent/private schools, 12, 68; secularization of public schools, 58–60. *See also* Catholics; faith-based schools; Protestants

citizenship development: Alberta's *Inspiring Education*, 78; Anglo-Canadian cultural dominance, 115; anti-bullying legislation, 59; Christian religious traditions, 58–9; common school model, 4; gay–straight alliance directives, 59; historical background, 21, 71–2

class, social. *See* social class

classroom practices and multiculturalism, 64–6

Coalition of Independent Homeschoolers, 81

Collins, R., 100

common school model: about, 3–4, 17–18; Anglo-Canadian cultural dominance, 4, 19, 115; assimilation of minority populations, 10, 19, 51–2; common culture, language, and community, 18, 24, 51–2, 54, 92; critique of, 18–19,

126–7; Dewey's influence, 72–3; diversity of society, 18, 24; historical background, 4, 18, 51–2; pluralism, 23–4; social cohesion, 4, 18, 19, 54, 115–16

communitarianism, 9, 16–19. *See also* common school model

concerted cultivation, 26–7

Constitution Act (1867): historical background, 43n1, 47, 48; language rights for francophones and anglophones, 33–5; provincial jurisdiction for education, 34, 35, 48; religious rights for Catholics and Protestants, 33–5

costs of school choice: about, 107–9; alternative programs, 90, 92, 107–9; bursaries, 134; elite specialist schools, 109, 133, 134, 139; extracurricular activities, 26, 109; inter- and intra-district choice, 14; neoliberal funding, 27–9, 110, 134–5, 136–7; as potential barrier, 26, 108–9, 139; subsidies for language programs, 105–6; transportation, 14, 26, 80(t), 90, 92, 107–8, 109; tutoring, 26, 109; uniforms, 26, 108–9; unpaid fees, 105–6

Daleney, C.F., 17

Davies, S. 82

Deaf community, 65(t), 132

decision making. *See* parental decision making

Developing and Implementing Equity and Inclusive Education Policies (Ontario), 57–8

Dewey, John, 72–3

difference principle (greatest benefit to least advantaged), 114, 128–9 digital technologies and online learning, 13, 78–9, 81, 83

disabilities, people with: accommodations for diversity, 57–8, 65–6; anti-bullying legislation, 59; Charter rights, 52, 69; Deaf community, 65(t), 132; historical background, 81; homeschooling, 81. *See also* special needs schools (programs)

disadvantaged and marginalized students: access to schools, 4, 5; accommodations for, 4, 64–6; Africentric schools, 64, 114, 124–5, 138; Alberta charter schools, 89, 93, 106, 136; alternative schools, 75, 93; difference principle (greatest benefit to least advantaged), 114, 128–9; elite specialist schools (sports or arts), 133–4, 139; equity funding, 137; historical background, 4, 10; liberal multiculturalism, 124–5; location of alternative schools, 12, 29, 104–5, 106, 111; myth of meritocracy, 94–6; weakening of local schools because of school choice, 5. *See also* Aboriginal education; accommodations for diversity; equality of opportunity; immigrant minority groups

diversity, accommodations for. *See* accommodations for diversity

Edmonton Public School Board, Alberta: Aboriginal schools, 40; alternative schools, 40, 61, 91, 102, 106, 130–1; faith-based schools, 61, 75, 130–1; heritage-language schools, 63, 75; historical background, 75, 91; location of

alternative schools, 106; middle-class anxiety, 102; open enrolment, 91

education, goals of. *See* goals of education policy

educational reform movements. *See* history of education policy

elite specialist schools (sports or arts): about, 110–11, 133–4; alternative schools, 102, 106; costs, 109, 133–4, 139; critique of, 110–11; disadvantaged students, 102, 110–11, 133–4, 139; equality of opportunity, 102, 109; gifted learners, 102, 103–4, 110–11; government regulation, 133–4; independent/private schools, 83; recommended ethical principles, 133–4, 137–9; supplementary activities, 109

elites, education for: historical background, 18–19, 71

English as a second language: Alberta charter schools, 61, 89, 106; Quebec's English-language schools, 67–8

English language and anglophones: about, 10; Anglo-Canadian cultural dominance, 4, 19, 51–2, 68, 115; Charter rights, 44, 49; Official Languages Act, 43–7, 49; rights under Constitution Act, 33–5; statistics on bilingualism, 46

enrolment, open. *See* open enrolment (intra-district)

equality of opportunity: about, 4, 10–11, 22–3, 109–11; alternative schools, 91–2; critique of, 15, 25–7; difference principle (greatest benefit to least advantaged), 114, 128–9; government regulations,

110; myth of meritocracy, 94–6;
provincial equalization policies, 7;
and social class, 22–3; strict equality, 128–9. *See also* liberal theory
ethical principles for policies: about,
11, 112–14, 137–9; communitarian common good, 17; difference
principle (greatest benefit to
least advantaged), 114, 128–9;
ethical individualism, 24, 114, 127;
government role, 31; individuals'
ability to make informed judgments, 127–8, 130; recommended
ethical principles, 137–9; research
on, 113. *See also* good life; liberal
multiculturalism; liberal theory
ethnic minority groups: about, 113,
116–17, 121–2; liberal multiculturalism, 116–17. *See also* immigrant
minority groups
Everdale Place, Toronto, 75
expressive liberty, 21–2

faith-based schools: about, 60–1,
62(t), 125–6, 129–31; as alternative
schools, 61, 62(t); autonomous individuals, 127–8, 130, 138; critique
of, 114–15, 125–6, 129–31; curriculum, 61, 62(t); excluded from
Charter rights, 60–1; funding,
60–1, 62(t), 125–6, 130–1, 138; in-
dependent/private schools, 12, 61,
68; liberal multiculturalism, 125–6;
limitations on, 62(t), 130, 138;
recommended ethical principles,
129–31, 137–9; statistics, 62(t)
Feinberg, W., 64
fine arts schools. *See* elite specialist
schools (sports or arts)

*First Nations Control of First Nations
Education* (AFN), 37–8, 42
First Nations Control of First Nations
Education Act (Bill C-33), 118–20
First Nations students. *See* Aboriginal
education
francophones. *See* French language
and francophones
Fraser Institute, 6, 77
French immersion schools (programs),
10, 45–9, 47(t)
French language and francophones:
about, 10, 117–18; Charter rights,
8, 44, 117–18; common school
model, 19; control by francophone parents, 46, 117; historical
background, 8–10, 67, 117; liberal
multiculturalism, 117–18; national
minority groups, 32–3, 116–17;
Official Languages Act, 43–7, 49;
Quebec's interculturalism, 10,
51, 66–9; recommended ethical
principles, 137–9; rights under
Constitution Act, 33–5, 118; statistics on bilingualism, 46
Friedman, Milton, 16, 27–8

Galston, W., 21–2, 127
GATE (Gifted and Talented
Education), Calgary, 103–4
gay students. *See* LGBT students
gender: accommodations for diversity, 57–8, 65–6; anti-bullying
legislation, 59; authentic recognition of diversity, 65; Charter rights,
52; gender separation of Muslim
students, 54, 57; and parental decision making, 25–6; single-gender
schools, 83, 102, 111

German language, 65(t), 122. *See also* heritage-language schools (programs)

gifted and talented students, 102, 103–4, 132

goals of education policy: about, 5–6, 30–1, 114; Aboriginal education, 38–40, 41–2; accommodation of diversity, 68–9; of alternative schools, 90–1; autonomous individuals, 20–1, 31; common good, 17, 30; homeschooling, 79, 81–2; and liberalism, 20–1; and neoliberalism-inspired reforms, 88–9, 93, 110; private *vs.* public good, 18–19, 30–1. *See also* good life; history of education policy

Goldthorpe, J., 99

good life: autonomous individuals, 20–1; in common school model, 24; in communitarianism, 17; in ethical individualism, 24, 114, 127; in liberal theory, 20–1, 127; private *vs.* public good, 18–19, 30–1; Rawls on, 21, 127–8

Gove, Michael, 7

government, provincial. *See* provincial and territorial governments

Greenhouse School, Regina, 75

Hall-Dennis Report, 74

Harper, Stephen, 42

Hebrew language. *See* Jewish students

heritage-language schools (programs): about, 63–4, 68–9, 122–3; Aboriginal immersion programs, 39–40; costs, 105–6; critique of, 63, 114–15, 122–3; funding summary, 65(t); historical background, 10, 75; Inuit languages, 39, 47; lack of federal protection, 63; liberal multiculturalism, 122–3; multiculturalism principles, 53–4, 63, 115; proficiency in dominant language, 123, 138; recommended ethical principles, 122–3, 137–9; research on, 123; tolerance and understanding, 63. *See also specific languages*

Hindu students, 56, 57

history of education policy: about, 10, 70–9; alternative schools, 75–6, 90; autonomous individuals, 21; Canadian Multiculturalism Act, 10, 53–5, 59, 63; child-centred approach, 72, 74, 75; common school model, 18; core disciplines movement, 73; Dewey's influence, 72–3; elite private schools, 18, 71; evaluation, 7–8, 77, 78; global knowledge-based economy, 76–7, 98, 100–1; government role, 21; neoliberal-inspired reforms, 76–7, 134–5; new provincial frameworks, 76–8; Official Languages Act, 43–7, 49; progressive movement, 72–3; recent trends, 77–9; reform movements, 10, 70–1, 76–7, 112; romantic progressivism, 73–5, 78–9, 81; Ryerson's influence, 71–4; school administration, 71–2; school choice options, 73, 74–5; technology, 73, 78–9. *See also* Canadian Charter of Rights and Freedoms (1982); Constitution Act (1867); philosophical frameworks

Hogben, Alia, 57

Holt, John, 79, 81

homeschooling: about, 13, 79–83, 92, 132–3; evaluation and testing, 82–3, 133; funding, 13n4, 80(t), 82; goals of, 79, 81–2; government regulation, 81–3, 130, 132–3; historical background, 77, 79, 81; liberal theory, 132–3; online learning, 13, 81; provincial summary, 80(t); recommended ethical principles, 132–3, 137–9; registration with school boards, 13, 82, 83, 133; religious focus, 61, 79, 82; statistics on, 13n4, 82; tension between state and parental responsibilities, 79, 81, 132–3; unschooling approach, 79, 81

human rights: historical background, 52

human rights charter. *See* Canadian Charter of Rights and Freedoms (1982)

Hutterite students, 12, 61, 129–31

immigrant minority groups: about, 10, 50–1, 116–17, 121–2; accommodations for diversity, 53–8, 65–6; Africentric schools, 64, 114, 124–5, 138; assimilation of, 10, 51–2; balance of individual *vs.* group rights, 68; Charter rights, 52, 54–5; as civic equals, 53; ethnic minority groups, 113, 116–17, 121–2; exit rights, 121–2; historical background, 51–2; liberal multiculturalism, 121–2, 124–5; Multiculturalism Act's impact on, 54–5; Quebec's interculturalism, 10, 51, 66–9; recommended ethical principles, 121–2, 137–9. *See also* accommodations for diversity;

Canadian Multiculturalism Act (1988); heritage-language schools (programs)

independent/private schools: about, 12–13, 83–5, 92; balance between individual rights and pluralism, 84; costs, 12, 13, 108; critique of, 82, 84, 88–9; for different philosophical orientation, 83, 131; elite preparatory schools, 83–4; funding, 80(t), 84, 85; goals of, 83–4; government regulation, 12–13, 67–8, 84–5; historical background, 74–5, 77, 83; homeschooling registrants, 82–3; moves into public system, 75, 85, 90; online learning, 83; provincial/territorial summary, 80(t), 86(t); Quebec's English-language schools, 67–8; religious focus, 12, 61, 68, 83, 88; research on, 88; statistics, 85, 86(t); uniforms, 108–9

Indian Act (1867), 35–6, 48. *See also* Aboriginal education

individual rights: about, 9, 16, 20–2; autonomous individuals, 20–1; balance between rights and pluralism, 54–5, 57, 84; balance of rights and liberties, 22, 27, 68; critique of, 25–7; ethical individualism, 24, 114, 127; exit rights, 121–2; expressive liberty, 21–2; historical background, 20–1; Rawls's theory, 21. *See also* liberal theory

Inspiring Education (Alberta), 78

interculturalism in Quebec, 10, 51, 66–9

inter-district school choice, 14

intra-district school choice. *See* open enrolment (intra-district)

Inuit, 9, 32, 35, 37, 39, 47, 116, 120–1.
    See also Aboriginal education
Islam. *See* Muslim students

Jackson, M., 99
Jewish Defence League, 57
Jewish students: alternative schools,
    75; double identity of students, 56;
    faith-based schools, 12, 56, 60–1,
    62(t), 69, 75, 126, 129–31; Hebrew
    language, 62(t), 63, 65(t), 75, 122,
    126; independent/private schools,
    68. *See also* faith-based schools
Johnson, D., 88
Jones, R. v., 130

Knowledge Matters (Government of
    Canada), 76
Kymlicka, W., 32, 50, 115–16, 126, 129

languages, official. *See* official
    languages
languages other than English and
    French: immersion programs,
    39–40, 64; lack of protection
    under Constitution and Charter,
    63; liberal multiculturalism,
    122–3; proficiency in dominant
    language, 123, 138; protection
    under Multiculturalism Act, 53.
    See also heritage-language schools
    (programs)
Lareau, A., 26
learning theories, alternative schools
    with different, 111, 131, 138–9
LGBT students: accommodations for
    diversity, 56–9, 64–6; anti-bullying
    legislation, 59; Charter rights, 51,
    69; double identity of students, 56;

parental control and controversial
    issues, 59–60; voluntary subcul-
    tures, 56, 59
liberal multiculturalism: about,
    113, 114–17; Aboriginal peoples,
    118–21; accommodations with exit
    rights, 121–2; Africentric schools,
    64, 114, 124–5; equality of citizens,
    115; ethnic minority groups, 113,
    116–17, 121–2; faith-based schools,
    125–6; francophones, 117–18; her-
    itage-language programs, 122–3;
    immigrant minority groups, 121–2;
    nation building with minority
    rights, 115–16; national minority
    groups, 32–3, 116–17; rejection of
    unitary nation-state model, 115
liberal theory: about, 9, 19–20, 126–9;
    autonomous individuals, 20–2,
    126; critique of, 25–7; difference
    principle (greatest benefit to least
    advantaged), 128–9; equality of
    opportunity, 9, 16, 19–20; ethical
    individualism, 24, 114, 127; faith-
    based schools, 129–31; goals for
    school policy, 126; individuals'
    ability to make informed judg-
    ments, 127–8; liberty, 19–20; limi-
    tations on school choice within,
    132–4; pluralism, 9, 16, 19–20,
    23–5; rational choice theory, 25–6,
    29; tolerance and understanding,
    19–20. *See also* equality of oppor-
    tunity; liberal multiculturalism;
    pluralism
Living and Learning (Hall-Dennis
    Report), 74
Locke, John, 20–1
Logos Society, Edmonton, 61, 130

lower-income families. *See* disadvantaged and marginalized students; social class
Lucey, H., 102–3

MacIntyre, A., 17
magnet schools. *See* alternative schools (programs)
Mahe v. Alberta, 46
mainstream schools. *See* public schools
Mandarin language, 63, 64, 65(t), 105–6, 122. *See also* heritage-language schools (programs)
Manitoba: Aboriginal education, 41; alternative schools, 61, 90; anglophone, francophone, and French immersion, 45–6, 47(t); faith-based schools, 61, 62(t), 125–6; heritage-language programs, 64, 65(t); homeschooling, 80(t); independent/private schools, 62(t), 80(t), 85, 86(t); open enrolment, 80(t), 90
marginalized students. *See* disadvantaged and marginalized students
Memorandum of Understanding for First Nations Education in Alberta, 41–2
Mendelson, M., 119–20
Mennonites, 12, 61
meritocracy and inequality, 94–6, 110–11
Metis students, 9, 32, 35, 37, 116. *See also* Aboriginal education
middle class: advantages of, 15, 22–3, 26; anxieties, 76, 94, 98, 100–4; Bourdieu's habitus, 97; concerted cultivation, 26–7; historical background, 76; intensive parenting, 26–7; myth of meritocracy, 94–6; parental decision making, 25–6,

101–2; reproduction of class advantage, 5, 26, 94–6. *See also* social class
Mi'kmaq students, 39, 41, 121
Mill, John Stuart, 20–1
minority groups. *See* ethnic minority groups; immigrant minority groups; national minority groups
Montessori schools, 83, 111, 131, 138
moral principles. *See* ethical principles for policies
Mother Earth's Children's Charter School, 40, 89, 106
multiculturalism: about, 51–5; anti-bullying legislation, 59; authentic recognition of diversity, 53–4, 64–6; balance of individual rights and pluralism, 24, 54–5, 57–8; bilingualism within, 52; Charter rights, 52, 54–5; classroom practices, 64–6; historical background, 51–2; languages other than English and French, 53; Multiculturalism Act, 10, 53–5, 59, 63; non-recognition as oppression, 53; pluralism, 16, 23–4, 54; principles of, 53–4; provincial variations, 54–5; recommended ethical principles, 137–9; rejection of unitary nation-state model, 115; secularization of public schools, 58–60; tolerance and understanding, 54, 64–5. *See also* accommodations for diversity; immigrant minority groups; liberal multiculturalism
Multiculturalism Act. *See* Canadian Multiculturalism Act (1988)
Muslim students: accommodations for diversity, 54, 56–8, 121; Alberta charter schools, 61, 89, 106;

faith-based schools, 60, 61, 62(t), 126, 129–31; independent/private schools, 12, 68. *See also* faith-based schools

National Indian Brotherhood, 37–8
national minority groups: about, 8–9, 32–3, 116–17; liberal multiculturalism, 116–17; recommended ethical principles, 137–9. *See also* Aboriginal education; Quebec and Quebecois
neighbourhood schools. *See* common school model
neighbourhood schools, attendance outside. *See* inter-district school choice; open enrolment (intra-district)
neoliberalism: about, 5n1, 16, 27–30, 114, 134–7; accountability, 28–9, 134–6; Alberta schools, 77, 85–9, 134–5; critique of, 5, 29–30, 135–7, 139; deregulation of government, 134; funding (vouchers, tuition credits), 27–9, 110, 134–5, 136–7; goals of education, 88–9, 110, 136; government policy, 28–30; historical background, 76–9; homogenous *vs.* diverse populations, 30; lack of ethical basis, 114, 135, 137; market forces, 4–5, 27–9, 30, 76, 85–6, 88–9, 93, 110–11, 134–5; Ontario schools, 134; parents as consumers, 28–30, 134–5; recommended ethical principles, 114, 137–9. *See also* charter schools, Alberta
New Brunswick: Aboriginal education, 41; anglophone, francophone, and French immersion,
44–6, 47(t); on continuum of school choice, 79; faith-based schools, 61, 62(t); heritage-language programs, 65(t); homeschooling, 80(t); independent/private schools, 80(t), 85, 86(t); new provincial framework, 77–8; only officially bilingual province, 47; open enrolment, 80(t)
New Zealand, 135
Newfoundland and Labrador: anglophone, francophone, and French immersion, 44–6, 47(t); on continuum of school choice, 79; faith-based schools, 61, 62(t); heritage-language programs, 65(t); homeschooling, 80(t); independent/private schools, 80(t), 86(t); open enrolment, 80(t); secular public system, 34
non-official languages. *See* heritage-language schools (programs); languages other than English and French
Northwest Territories: anglophone, francophone, and French immersion, 47(t); on continuum of school choice, 79; heritage-language programs, 65(t); homeschooling, 80(t); independent/private schools, 80(t); no funding for faith-based schools, 62(t); official status of Aboriginal languages, 47; open enrolment, 80(t)
Nova Scotia: anglophone, francophone, and French immersion, 45–6, 47(t); on continuum of school choice, 79; faith-based schools, 61, 62(t); heritage-language programs, 65(t);

homeschooling, 80(t); independent/private schools, 80(t), 86(t); Mi'kmaq students, 39, 41, 121; open enrolment, 80(t)

Nunavut: anglophone, francophone, and French immersion, 47(t); on continuum of school choice, 79; heritage-language programs, 65(t), 120–1; historical background, 39; homeschooling, 80(t); independent/private schools, 80(t); Inuit education, 39, 120–1; liberal multiculturalism, 120–1; no funding for faith-based schools, 62(t); official languages, 39, 47; open enrolment, 80(t)

official languages: about, 10, 33, 43–7; anglophones in Quebec, 33; francophones outside Quebec, 33; French in Quebec, 47; historical background, 43–4, 52; Inuktitut in Nunavut, 39, 47; within multiculturalism, 52, 68–9; Official Languages Act, 43–7, 49. *See also* English language and anglophones; French language and francophones

online learning, 13, 78–9, 81, 83

Ontario: accommodations for diversity, 56–8, 64–5, 68–9; Africentric schools, 64, 124–5; alternative schools, 90–1; anglophone, francophone, and French immersion, 45–6, 47(t); anti-bullying legislation, 59; balance of individual *vs.* group rights, 68; Catholic and Protestant schools, 34–5, 62(t), 125; Constitutional rights for Catholic schools, 34, 125;

faith-based schools, 60–1, 62(t), 125–6; francophone separate schools, 46–7; gay–straight alliance directives, 59; Hall-Dennis Report, 74; heritage-language programs, 65(t); historical background, 71–2, 71–4; homeschooling, 80(t), 83; independent/private schools, 80(t), 83–5, 86(t); neoliberal-inspired reforms, 134; open enrolment, 80(t), 90; research by think tanks, 6n2; romantic progressivism, 73; Ryerson's influence, 71–4

Ontario, Adler v., 60–1

open enrolment (intra-district): about, 14, 89–92; provincial summary, 80(t); support for parental decision making, 91; transportation costs, 14, 80(t)

Palliser Regional School Division, Alberta, 61

Palmater, P., 119

parents: concerted cultivation, 26–7; credential society, 100–1; expressive liberty, 21–2; and global knowledge-based economy, 4, 76–7, 98, 100–1; intensive parenting, 26–7, 82, 110; middle-class anxiety, 76, 94, 98, 100–4; as neoliberal consumers, 28–30, 134–5; parental control and controversial issues, 59–60; parent-based school councils, 87, 134–5; tension between state and parental rights, 21–2, 79

parental decision making: about, 10–11, 96–100, 110–11; access to information, 25–6, 28, 91; active and inactive choosers, 99–100; Bourdieu's habitus, 97, 99; choice theories, 25–6, 29, 98–9; common school model, 23–4; costs and benefits, 99; location of alternative schools, 104–5; parent resources for, 6, 91; as social process, 25–6, 96–7, 98–9, 101

performing arts schools. *See* elite specialist schools (sports or arts)

philosophical frameworks: about, 6–9, 15–16, 77–8; communitarianism, 9, 16–19; ethical individualism, 24, 114, 127; historical background, 77–8; influence of think tanks, 6, 77; terminology, 15–16. *See also* communitarianism; liberal multiculturalism; liberal theory; neoliberalism

philosophical orientations, alternative schools with different, 111, 131, 138–9

pluralism: about, 16, 23–4; balance between individual rights and pluralism, 24, 54–5, 57–8, 82; Quebec's interculturalism, 66–9. *See also* liberal theory; multiculturalism

Prince Edward Island: Aboriginal education, 41; anglophone, francophone, and French immersion, 45–6, 47(t); on continuum of school choice, 79; faith-based schools, 61, 62(t); heritage-language programs, 65(t); home-schooling, 80(t); independent/private schools, 80(t), 85, 86(t); open enrolment, 80(t)

private schools. *See* independent/private schools

Programme for International Student Assessment (PISA), 8

Protestants: Aboriginal education, 36–7; alternative schools, 61; historical background, 33–5; home-schooling, 79, 80(t); prayers in public schools, 58–9; rights under Constitution Act, 33–5, 48, 60; secularization of public schools, 58–60. *See also* faith-based schools

provincial and territorial governments: accommodations for diversity, 54–8, 68–9; jurisdiction for education under Constitution Act, 34, 35, 48, 70; jurisdiction for Inuit, Metis, and non-status Indians, 35–6; language rights under Constitution Act, 33–5; religious rights under Constitution Act, 33–5

public schools: about, 12; Aboriginal partnerships, 40; loss of student diversity in school choice, 30; secularization of, 58–60. *See also* common school model

public schools, specialized. *See* alternative schools (programs); elite specialist schools (sports or arts); faith-based schools; heritage-language schools (programs); special needs schools (programs)

Punjabi language, 62(t), 63, 64

Quebec and Quebecois: Aboriginal education, 41; accommodations for diversity, 55–6, 66–9; alternative schools, 90; anglophones, francophones, and French immersion, 44–6, 47(t); anglophones in Protestant school systems, 34–5; Charter rights, 44, 48; control over education under Constitution

Act, 34, 48; cultural vulnerability of francophones, 67; faith-based schools, 34–5, 62(t), 125–6; heritage-language programs, 65(t); historical background, 43–4; homeschooling, 80(t); increase in educational control, 32; independent/private schools, 62(t), 67–8, 80(t), 83–5, 86(t); interculturalism, 10, 51, 66–9; language enrolment requirements, 44–5; liberal multiculturalism, 117–18; as national minority groups, 32–3, 116–17; officially unilingual, 47; open enrolment, 80(t), 90; recommended ethical principles, 137–9; rejection of multiculturalism, 51; research by think tanks, 6n2; resistance to multiculturalism, 69. *See also* French language and francophones; national minority groups

R. v. Jones, 130
race and ethnicity: accommodations for diversity, 57–8, 64–6; anti-bullying legislation, 59; Charter rights, 52; and parental decision making, 25–6. *See also* accommodations for diversity; immigrant minority groups
rational choice theory, 25–6, 29
Rawls, John, 21, 23, 114, 127–30, 138
Reay, D., 102–3
reform movements. *See* history of education policy
Reggio Emilia, 83, 131
Reich, R., 24, 126
religious minority groups: about, 10, 50–1; accommodations for

diversity, 54–8, 60, 64–6; alternative schools, 61; Charter rights, 52, 55–6, 58, 69; double identity of students, 56; historical background, 33–5, 79; parental control and controversial issues, 59–60; prayers in public schools, 56–9; religious symbols (Sikh), 55–6, 66; rights under Constitution Act, 33–5, 48; secularization of public schools, 58–60. *See also* faith-based schools; *and specific religions*
residential school system, 36–7, 41–2, 48
The Rise of Meritocracy (Young), 95n1
Roman Catholics. *See* Catholics
Ryerson, Edgerton, 71–4

St. Norbert's Community School, Winnipeg, 75
Sandel, M., 17
Saskatchewan: Aboriginal education, 41; alternative schools, 61; anglophone, francophone, and French immersion, 45–6, 47(t); Catholic and Protestant schools, 34–5, 62(t), 125; Constitutional rights for Catholic schools, 34, 125; faith-based schools, 61, 62(t), 125–6; heritage-language programs, 64, 65(t); homeschooling, 80(t), 83; independent/private schools, 62(t), 80(t), 85, 86(t); open enrolment, 80(t)
Saskatoon Tribal Council, 41
Saturday School, Calgary, 75
school choice: about, 3–4, 11–14, 31; admission policies, 111; American influences on, 7–8; debates on, 4–9; defined, 3, 11; goals of, 30–1;

government role, 31, 109–11; hierarchy of disciplines, 11, 107; provincial and territorial summary, 79, 80(t); public and private, as concepts, 15–16; recent trends, 78–9; research on, 5–7; terminology on, 11–14. *See also* equality of opportunity; ethical principles for policies; goals of education policy; philosophical frameworks

second language, English as a. *See* English as a second language

second-language immersion programs, 39–40, 64. *See also* French immersion schools (programs); heritage-language schools (programs)

sexual orientation. *See* LGBT students

sexuality: parental control and controversial issues, 59–60

Sikh students, 55–6, 66

social class: accommodations for diversity, 57–8; Bourdieu's habitus, 97; myth of meritocracy, 94–6; parental decision making, 25–6, 96–7, 98–9, 102–3; reproduction of social class, 5, 26, 94–6; research on, 5; and school choice, 109–11; uniforms, 108–9; values and socialization, 97; working-class parents, 99, 102–3. *See also* disadvantaged and marginalized students; middle class

social justice: common school model, 4, 28; historical background, 52; neoliberal critique of, 28. *See also* Canadian Charter of Rights and Freedoms (1982); disadvantaged and marginalized students

Society for the Advancement of Excellence in Education, 6, 77

Spanish language, 63, 64, 65(t), 122. *See also* heritage-language schools (programs)

special needs schools (programs): about, 131–2; accommodations for diversity, 65–6; Alberta charter schools, 89; Charter rights, 52, 69; Deaf community, 132; gifted learners, 102, 103–4, 132; homeschooling, 81; inter- and intra-district choice, 14; recommended ethical principles, 131–2, 137–9

specialized schools. *See* alternative schools (programs); elite specialist schools (sports or arts); heritage-language schools (programs); special needs schools (programs)

sports academies. *See* elite specialist schools (sports or arts)

Sudbury Board of Education, Zylberberg v., 58–9

Summerhill-inspired schools, 131

Supreme Court decisions: equality of funding for French-language schools, 118; francophone control of school boards, 46; government control over homeschooling, 130; limitations on faith-based schools, 60–1, 130; Sikh dagger accommodation, 55–6, 66

Talmud Torah Society, Edmonton, 61, 75

tax credits, 110

Taylor, A., 98–100

Taylor, C., 16

technologies and online learning, 13, 78–9, 81, 83

think tanks, 6, 77

Toronto District School Board: accommodations for diversity, 56–8, 64–5, 124–5; Africentric schools, 64, 124–5; alternative schools, 75; LGBT students, 56n1, 64

Tory, John, 125

Trans-Davies, N., 78–9

transgender students. *See* LGBT students

Trudeau, Pierre, 43–4, 47, 52

Ukrainian language, 63, 65(t), 116, 122. *See also* heritage-language schools (programs)

uniforms, 108–9

United Kingdom: educational reform movement, 76; myth of meritocracy, 95–6; neoliberal-inspired reforms, 135; parental decision making, 102–3; school choice research, 7

United States: charter schools, 136; Dewey's influence, 72–3; influence on Canadian policies, 7–8, 70; neoliberal-inspired reforms, 76, 135–6; parental decision making, 98; school choice policies, 7–8, 112

unofficial languages. *See* languages other than English and French

Valley Park Middle School, Toronto, 56

Van Pelt, N.D., 82

Vancouver: Aboriginal alternative schools, 40; faith-based schools, 62(t), 126; funding for French-language schools, 118

Victoria School of the Arts, Edmonton, 106

vouchers, school, 27–8, 110

vulnerable students. *See* disadvantaged and marginalized students

Waldorf schools, 83, 111, 131

weighted funding, 110

Weinstein, Meir, 57

Wilson, T., 15

Woollard, L., 98–100

working-class families, 71, 99, 102–3. *See also* social class

Wright, E.O., 96–7

Wu, J., 123

Wynne, Kathleen, 125

Young, Michael, 95

Yukon: anglophone, francophone, and French immersion, 47(t); on continuum of school choice, 79; heritage-language programs, 65(t); homeschooling, 80(t); independent/private schools, 80(t); no funding for faith-based schools, 62(t); open enrolment, 80(t)

Zine, J., 56

Zylberberg v. Sudbury Board of Education, 58–9